Family Favorite QUILTS

This eye-catching collection of mostly bed-size quilts has a lot of history behind it! In fact, you could say it has taken decades for several of these new quilts to evolve from Tammy Tadd's family history. Read the little anecdotes we've included as you create your own quilted beauties, and see if you don't feel right at home with Tammy and her fun-loving, affectionate folks.

MEET THE DESIGNER

Tammy Tadd is blessed with a family whose support and encouragement inspire her to create dozens of original quilts.

"It was my mother," Tammy says, "who never let me feel that anything was beyond my capability."

"Mom and I have always done well at hand work, including sewing, painting, and crafting." Tammy says. "Mom has quilted for over 20 years."

This "we can do it" attitude goes back another generation to Tammy's Grandma Bessie, who taught it to Tammy's mother.

"When Mom and I decided to market our quilting patterns, our first designs were called 'The Grandma Bessie Series.' Grandma went to be with the Lord several years ago, but she is still close to our hearts.

"Other pattern themes we have done are our regular Tammy Tadd Designs, Sunday Sampler Series, and Taddpoles Children's Series."

With five children of her own, Tammy finds that creating quilt patterns allows her to be a full-time mom. Gary, her husband, assists by designing pattern packages.

"Gary and I met at church," Tammy explains, "We have always shared the same faith and family values. I hope everyone will enjoy the stories and memories behind these quilts."

LEISURE ARTS, INC.
Little Rock, Arkansas

Cranberry Bowl

For holiday meals, Grandma Bessie always served her special cranberry sauce in a bowl of pink frosted glass with flowers painted on the side. What made the sauce special was the addition of applesauce and sugar, a recipe that pleased the children. Tammy says the flowers wore off that pink bowl a long time ago, but the family still treasures it, and it was the inspiration for this beautiful quilt. The pattern could easily be adjusted to a lap-size or crib-size quilt.

Cranberry Bowl

Made by Velda Grubbs
Finished Block Size: 16" x 16" (41 cm x 41 cm)
Finished Quilt Size: 87" x 103" (221 cm x 262 cm)

Yardage Requirements

Yardage is based on 45"w fabric.

- 7¼ yds (6.6 m) of antique ivory print
- 2½ yds (2.3 m) of cranberry print
- ¾ yd (69 cm) of light pink print
- ¾ yd (69 cm) **each** of 8 assorted pink and rose prints
- 1 yd (91 cm) of dark green print
- ¼ yd (23 cm) of medium green print
- 1 yd (91 cm) of binding fabric
- 8 yds (7.2 m) of backing fabric
- 120" x 120" (3.0 m x 3.0 m) batting

Cutting out the Backgrounds and Borders

*All measurements include a ¼" seam allowance. Follow **Rotary Cutting**, page 49, and **Adding Squared Borders**, page 54, to cut fabric.*

From antique ivory print:

- Cut 10 strips 16½" wide. From these strips, cut 20 squares (No. 1) 16½" x 16½" for background blocks.
- Cut 2 lengthwise strips (No. 2) 10½" x 82½" for outer side borders.
- Cut 2 lengthwise strips (No. 3) 10½" x 86½" for outer top and bottom borders.

From cranberry print:

- Cut 2 lengthwise strips (No. 4) 1½" x 80½" for inner side borders.
- Cut 2 lengthwise strips (No. 5) 1½" x 66½" for inner top and bottom borders.

Cutting the Appliqués

*Refer to **Making Templates**, page 52, to use patterns, pages 8-9, to make templates and to **Making Continuous Bias Binding**, page 57. Note: Appliqué patterns provided do not include seam allowances and are not reversed. If you use fusible web for the appliqués, the patterns should be reversed. Measurements given for bias strips include a ¼" seam allowance. To help keep blocks organized, lay out all appliqué pieces with corresponding backgrounds as you cut.*

From light pink print:

- Cut 20 circles on fold (B).

From medium green print:

- Cut 64 leaves (C).
- Cut 20 leaves (D).
- Cut 20 leaves (E).

From dark green print:

- Cut 68 leaves (C).
- Cut 16 leaves (D).
- Cut 28 leaves (E).
- Cut 24 flower bases (R).
- Cut 5 yds of 1"w continuous bias strip for 8 vines and 9 stems.

From assorted pink and rose prints:

- Cut 320 Template A's.
- Cut 40 flowers (F).
- Cut 40 **each** of flower centers (G and H).
- Cut 36 flowers (I).
- Cut 36 flower centers (J).
- Cut 12 **each** of flower petals (K, L, M, and N).
- Cut 12 flower centers (O).
- Cut 24 flowers (P).
- Cut 24 flower petals (Q).

Making the Blocks

*Follow **Piecing and Pressing**, page 51, and **Machine Appliqué**, page 52, to make the blocks. Refer to photo, page 4, and **Block Diagram** for placement. Working in alphabetical order, position pieces, then pin or baste in place on background square before appliquéing.*

1. Sew 16 A's of assorted prints together as shown to make **Unit 1**. Make 20 **Unit 1's**.

Unit 1
(make 20)

2. Center **Unit 1** on No. 1 background block and use **Mock Hand Appliqué**, page 53, to appliqué outer edge in place.

3. Position light pink print circle (B) on **Unit 1** as shown and appliqué in place to make **Unit 2**. Make 20 **Unit 2's**.

Unit 2
(make 20)

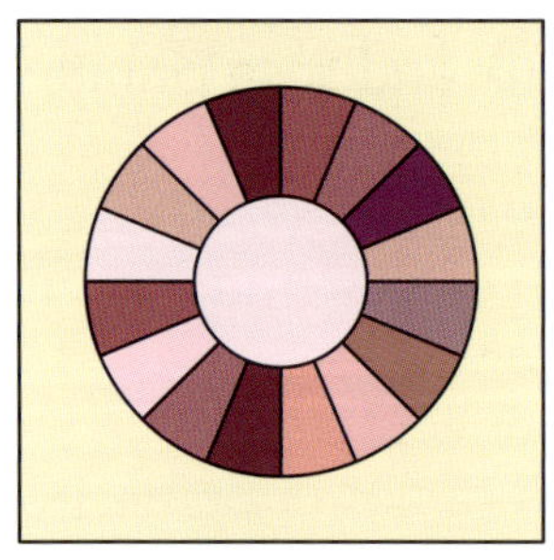

4. Use **Satin Stitch Appliqué**, page 53, to appliqué 1 medium green print leaf (C) and 1 dark green print leaf (C), flower (F) and flower centers (G and H) to center of circle (B) as shown to complete block. Make 20 blocks.

Block Diagram
(make 20)

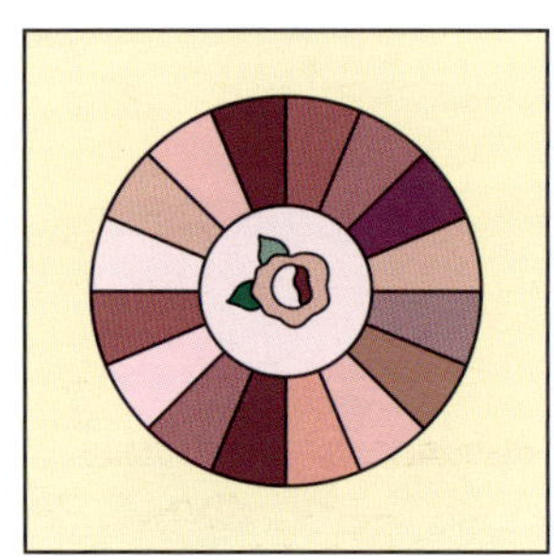

Assembling the Quilt Top

*Follow **Piecing and Pressing**, page 51, **Adding Squared Borders**, page 54, and **Machine Appliqué**, page 52, to make the quilt top. Refer to photo, page 4, and **Quilt Top Diagram** for placement. Working in alphabetical order, position pieces, then pin or baste in place on background squares before appliquéing.*

1. Sew the 20 blocks together in 5 rows of 4 blocks to make Quilt Top Center.

2. Use **Satin Stitch Appliqué**, page 53, to appliqué a dark green print leaf (C), a flower (I) and a flower center (J) over the intersection of every 4 blocks for a total of 12 flower appliqués (**Fig. 1**).

Fig. 1

Adding the Borders

*Follow **Piecing and Pressing**, page 51, **Adding Squared Borders**, page 54, and **Machine Appliqué**, page 52, to make the quilt top. Refer to **Corner Appliqué Diagram** and photo, page 4, for placement.*

1. Sew No. 4 inner side borders, then No. 5 inner top and bottom borders to Quilt Top Center.

2. Sew No. 2 outer side borders, then No. 3 outer top and bottom borders to pieced center.

3. For scalloped corners, place dashed line of scalloped corner pattern on fold of tracing paper. Trace pattern onto tracing paper and cut out.

4. Trace the scalloped corners onto quilt top. **Note:** If you will be machine quilting, do not cut out the scalloped corners until quilting has been completed.

5. Use **Satin Stitch Appliqué**, page 53, to appliqué vines, stems, 20 leaves (C), 9 leaves (D), 10 leaves (E), 5 flowers (F), 5 each of flower centers (G and H), 6 flowers (I), 6 flower centers (J), 3 each of flower petals (K, L, M, and N), 3 flower centers (O), 6 flowers (P), 6 flower petals (Q), and 6 flower bases (R) to each corner of the outer border to complete quilt top.

Completing the Quilt

1. Follow **Quilting**, page 54, to mark, layer, and quilt as desired. Our quilt was machine quilted.

2. Cut a 36" square of binding fabric. Follow **Making Continuous Bias Strip Binding**, page 57, to make $10^7/_8$ yds of $2^1/_2$"w binding.

3. Follow Steps 1 and 2 of **Attaching Binding with Mitered Corners**, page 58, to pin binding to front of quilt. Sew binding to quilt, easing curves and leaving a 2" overlap. Trim off excess binding and stitch overlap in place. Fold binding over to quilt backing and pin in place, covering stitching line. Blind stitch binding to backing.

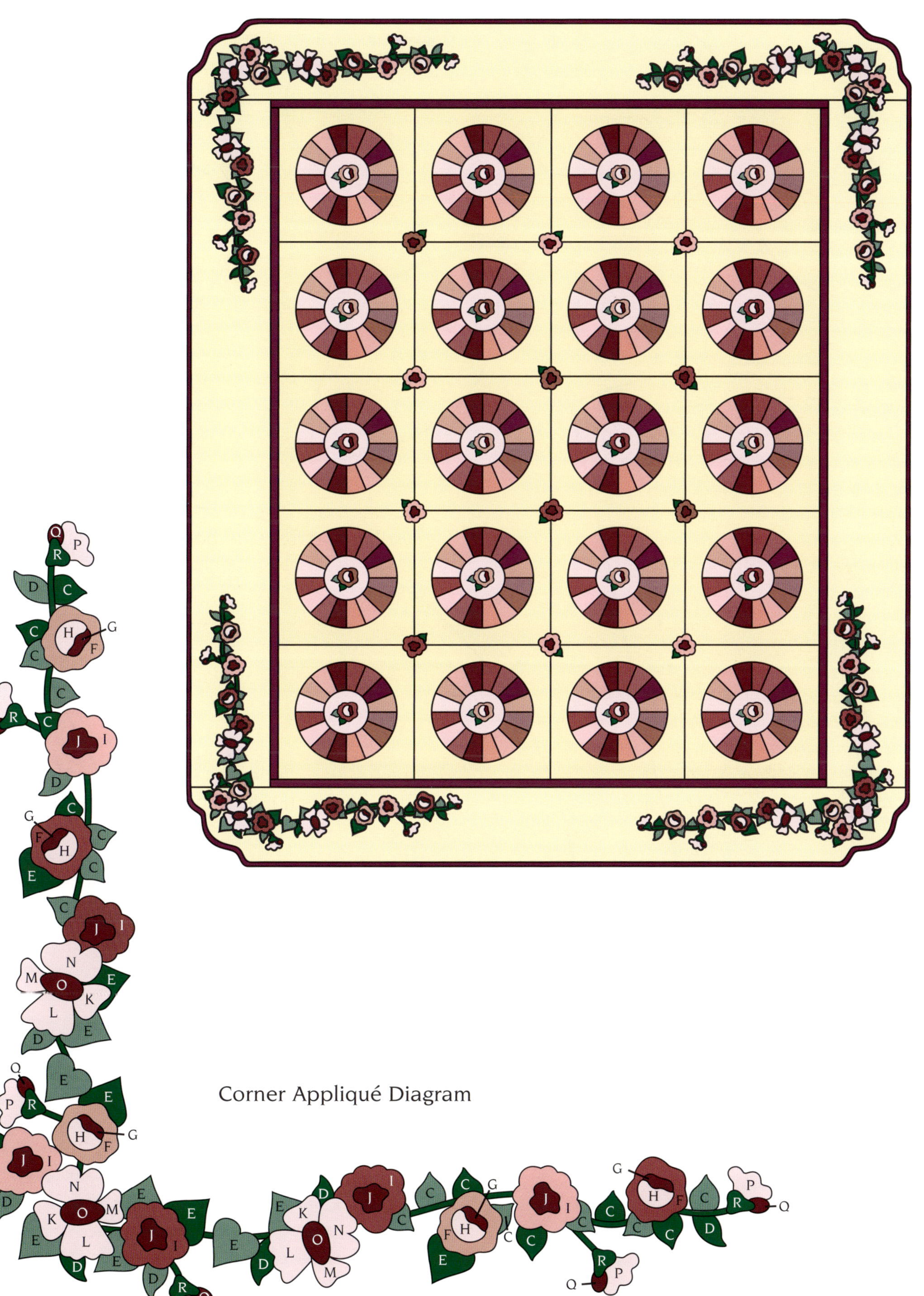

Corner Appliqué Diagram

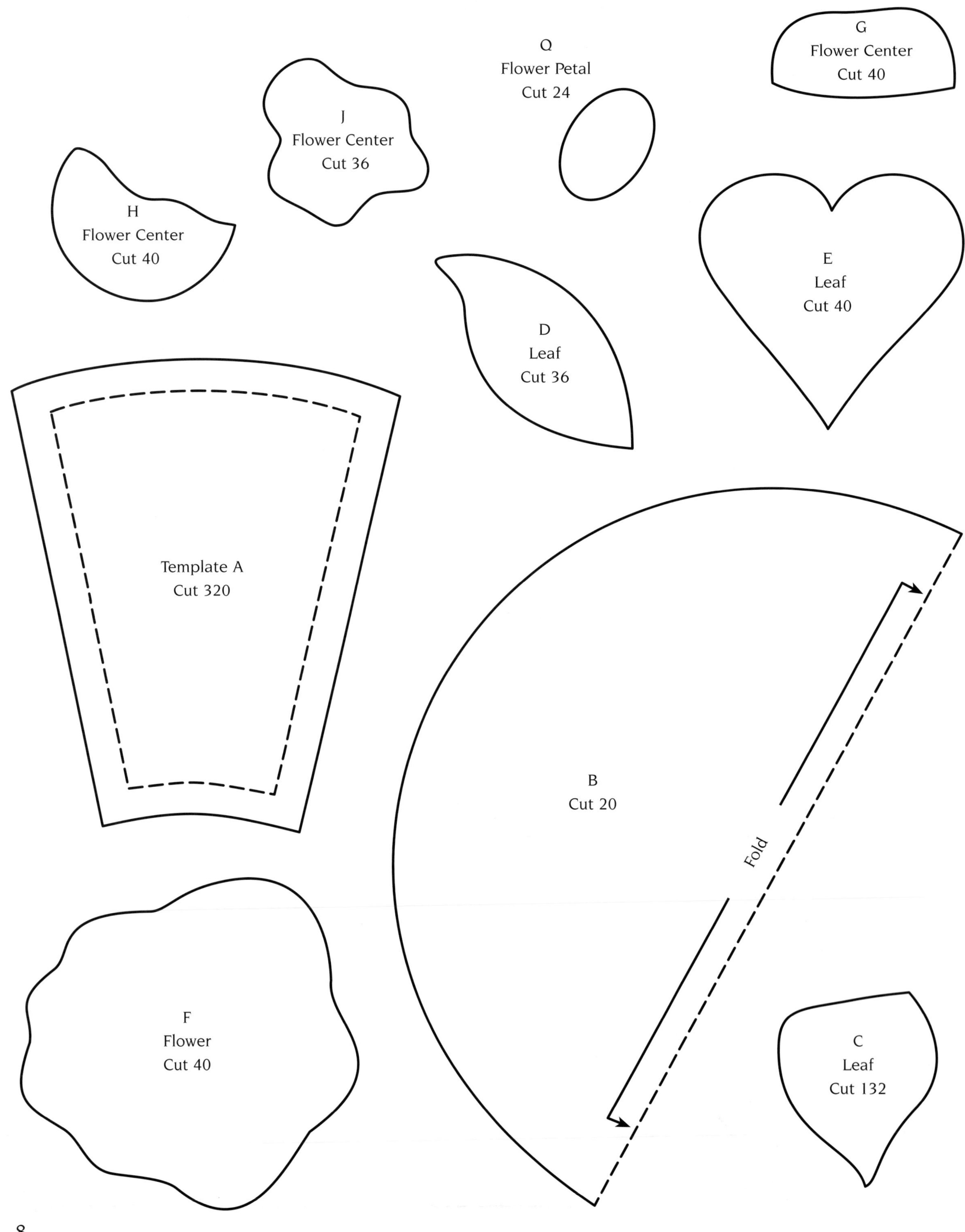

Q
Flower Petal
Cut 24
G
Flower Center
Cut 40
J
Flower Center
Cut 36
H
Flower Center
Cut 40
E
Leaf
Cut 40
D
Leaf
Cut 36
Template A
Cut 320
B
Cut 20
Fold
F
Flower
Cut 40
C
Leaf
Cut 132

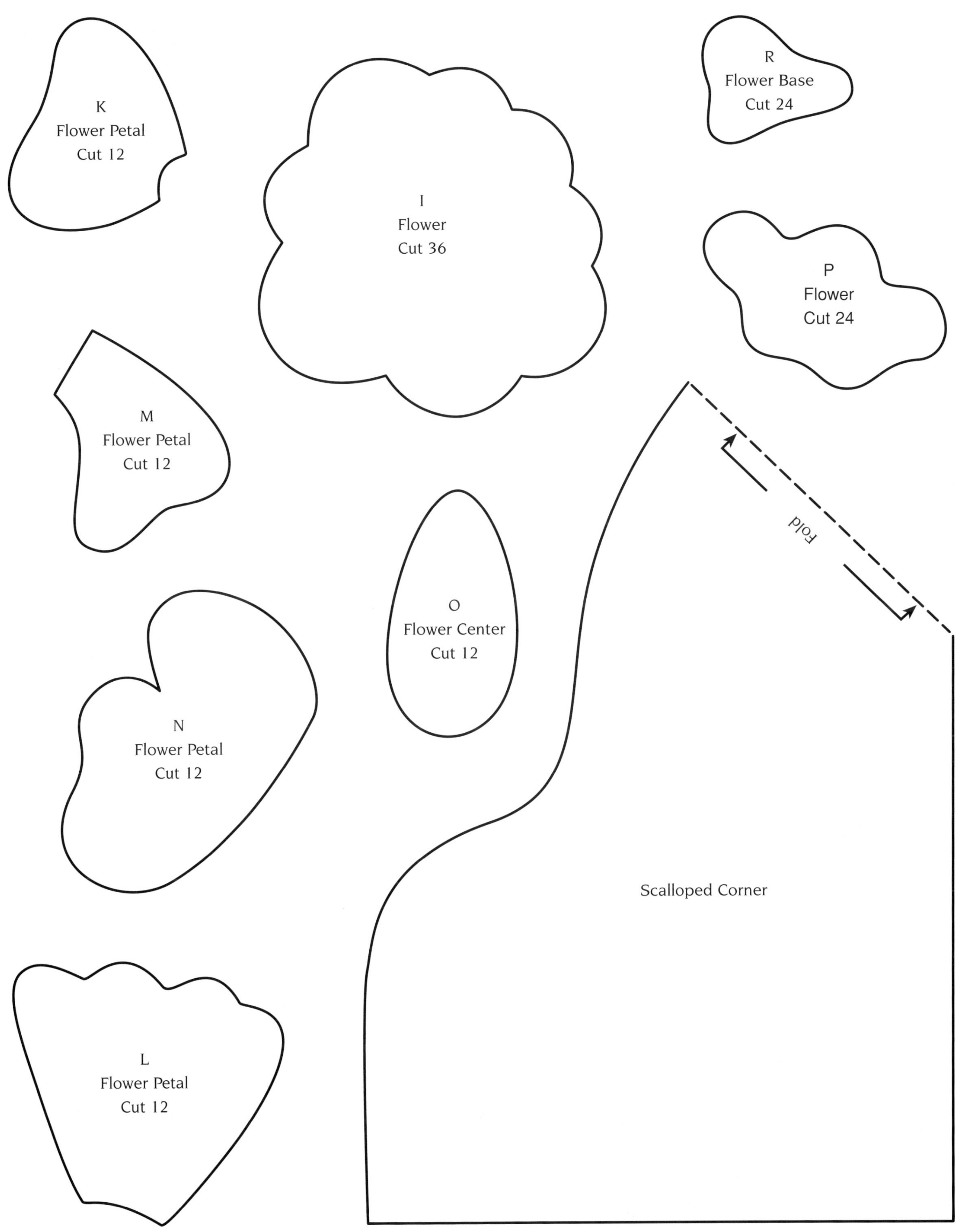

K
Flower Petal
Cut 12

I
Flower
Cut 36

R
Flower Base
Cut 24

P
Flower
Cut 24

M
Flower Petal
Cut 12

O
Flower Center
Cut 12

N
Flower Petal
Cut 12

Fold

Scalloped Corner

L
Flower Petal
Cut 12

Grandma's New Dress

Tammy says the reproduction fabrics in this bed-size quilt remind her of her Grandma Bessie, who, decades ago, had to be convinced to buy a bright, salmon-colored dress. Her reluctance may have been because of her husband's habit of pinching pennies. Grandma Bessie hid the bright-colored dress in her closet for weeks before wearing it. That way, when asked if the dress was new, she could reply, "Oh, Oliver, this has been hanging in the back of my closet."

Grandma's New Dress

Made by Tammy Tadd
Finished Block Size: 12" x 12" (31 cm x 31 cm)
Finished Quilt Size: 86" x 101" (218 cm x 257 cm)

Yardage Requirements

Yardage is based on 45"w fabric.

- $4^3/_8$ yds (4.0 m) of cream solid
- $2^1/_2$ yds (2.3 m) of pink solid
- $3/_4$ yd (69 cm) of lavender solid
- $1/_2$ yd (46 cm) of green solid
- $3/_8$ yd (34 cm) **each** of yellow, peach, and blue solids
- $1/_8$ yd (11 cm) **each** of dark pink, dark green, dark lavender, dark yellow, dark peach, and dark blue prints
- $3/_8$ yd (34 cm) **each** of light pink and light green prints
- $1/_4$ yd (23 cm) **each** of light lavender, light yellow, light peach, and light blue prints
- $3/_4$ yd (69 cm) of binding fabric
- 8 yds (7.3 m) of backing fabric
- 120" x 120" (3.0 m x 3.0 m) batting

Cutting out the Pieces

All measurements include a $1/_4$" seam allowance. Follow **Rotary Cutting**, *page 49, and* **Adding Squared Borders**, *page 54, to cut fabric.*

From cream solid:
- Cut 2 lengthwise strips (A) $8^1/_2$" x $84^1/_2$" for outer side borders.
- Cut 2 lengthwise strips (B) $8^1/_2$" x $85^1/_2$" for outer top and bottom borders.
- Cut 17 strips $3^1/_2$" wide. From these strips, cut 49 rectangles (C) $3^1/_2$" x $12^1/_2$" for sashings.

From pink solid:
- Cut 2 lengthwise strips (D) $3^1/_2$" x $78^1/_2$" for inner side borders.
- Cut 2 lengthwise strips (E) $3^1/_2$" x $69^1/_2$" for inner top and bottom borders.
- From remaining width, cut 5 strips $3^7/_8$" wide. From these strips, cut 32 squares $3^7/_8$" x $3^7/_8$". Cut each square once diagonally to make 64 triangles (F).

From lavender solid:
- Cut 3 strips $3^1/_2$" wide. From these strips, cut 30 squares (G) $3^1/_2$" x $3^1/_2$" for setting squares.
- Cut 3 strips $3^7/_8$" wide. From these strips, cut 24 squares $3^7/_8$" x $3^7/_8$". Cut each square once diagonally to make 48 triangles (F).

From green solid:
- Cut 4 strips $3^7/_8$" wide. From these strips, cut 32 squares $3^7/_8$" x $3^7/_8$". Cut each square once diagonally to make 64 triangles (F).

From each yellow, peach, and blue solid:
- Cut 3 strips $3^7/_8$" wide. From these strips, cut 24 squares $3^7/_8$" x $3^7/_8$". Cut each square once diagonally to make 48 triangles (F).

From each dark green and dark pink print:
- Cut 1 strip $3^7/_8$" wide. From this strip, cut 8 squares $3^7/_8$" x $3^7/_8$". Cut each square once diagonally to make 16 triangles (H).

From each dark lavender, dark yellow, dark peach and dark blue print:
- Cut 1 strip $3^7/_8$" wide. From this strip, cut 6 squares $3^7/_8$" x $3^7/_8$". Cut each square once diagonally to make 12 triangles (H).

From each light green and light pink print:
- Cut 3 strips $3^7/_8$" wide. From these strips, cut 24 squares $3^7/_8$" x $3^7/_8$". Cut each square once diagonally to make 48 triangles (I).

From each light lavender, light yellow, light peach, and light blue print:
- Cut 2 strips $3^7/_8$" wide. From these strips, cut 18 squares $3^7/_8$" x $3^7/_8$". Cut each square once diagonally to make 36 triangles (I).

From binding fabric:
- Cut 10 strips $2^1/_2$"w.

Making the Blocks

Follow **Piecing and Pressing**, *page 51, to make the blocks.*

1. Sew a solid triangle (F) and a dark print triangle (H) together as shown to make **Unit 1**. Make 80 **Unit 1's** (16 each of green and pink; 12 each of lavender, yellow, peach, and blue).

Unit 1
(make 80)

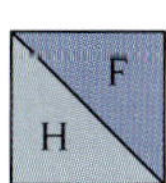

2. Sew 2 **Unit 1**'s of like color together as shown to make **Unit 2.** Make 40 **Unit 2**'s.

Unit 2
(make 40)

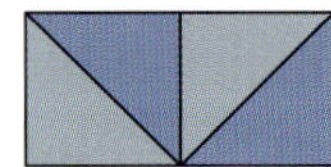

3. Sew 2 **Unit 2**'s of like color together as shown to make **Unit 3**. Make 20 **Unit 3**'s (4 each of pink and green; 3 each of lavender, yellow, peach, and blue).

Unit 3
(make 20)

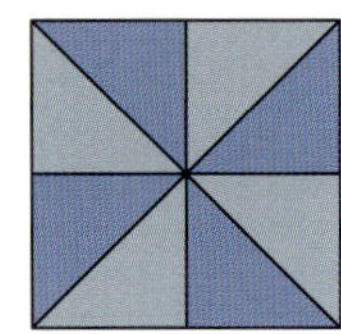

4. Sew a solid triangle (F) and a light print triangle (I) together as shown to make **Unit 4**. Make 240 **Unit 4**'s (48 each of green and pink; 36 each of lavender, yellow, peach, and blue).

Unit 4
(make 240)

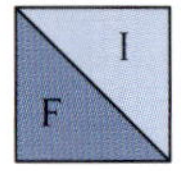

5. Sew 2 **Unit 4**'s of like color together as shown to make **Unit 5**. Make 40 **Unit 5**'s.

Unit 5
(make 40)

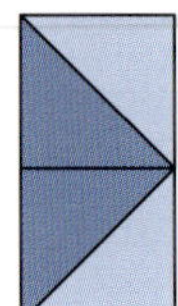

6. Sew 2 **Unit 5**'s to **Unit 3** as shown to make **Unit 6**. Make 20 **Unit 6**'s.

Unit 6
(make 20)

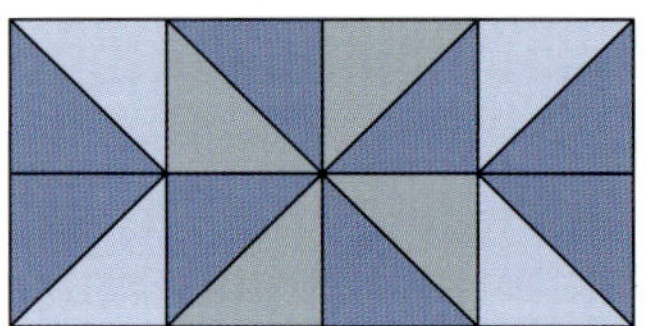

7. Sew 4 **Unit 4**'s of like color together as shown to make **Unit 7**. Make 40 **Unit 7**'s.

Unit 7
(make 40)

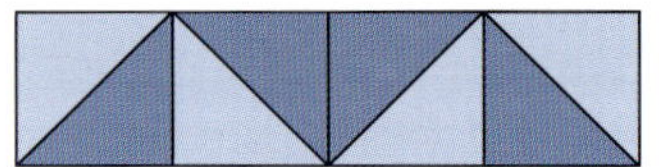

8. Sew 2 **Unit 7**'s to the top and bottom of **Unit 6** as shown to make block. Make 20 **Blocks**.

Block Diagram
(make 20)

Assembling the Quilt Top

Follow **Piecing and Pressing,** *page 51, to make the quilt top. Refer to photo, page 12, and* **Quilt Top Diagram** *for placement.*

1. Sew 5 lavender setting squares (G) and 4 cream sashing strips (C) together to make **Unit 8**. Make 6 **Unit 8**'s.
2. Sew 5 cream sashing strips (C) and 4 **Blocks** together to make **Unit 9**. Make 5 **Unit 9**'s.
3. Sew **Unit 8**'s and **Unit 9**'s together to make Quilt Top Center.

Adding the Borders

Follow **Piecing and Pressing,** *page 51, and* **Adding Squared Borders,** *page 54, to add the borders. Refer to photo, page 12, and* **Quilt Top Diagram** *for placement.*

1. Sew pink inner side borders (D), then pink inner top and bottom borders (E) to Quilt Top Center.
2. Sew cream outer side borders (A), then cream outer top and bottom borders (B) to **pieced center** to make quilt top.

Completing the Quilt

1. Follow **Quilting,** page 54, to mark, layer, and quilt as desired. Our quilt was machine quilted.
2. Follow **Making Straight Grain Binding,** page 58, to make $10^3/_4$ yds of $2^1/_2$"w binding.
3. Follow **Attaching Binding with Mitered Corners,** page 58, to attach binding to quilt.

Quilt Top Diagram

Les Femmes Rouge

Les Femmes Rouge (The Red Ladies) was designed from Tammy's love of toile fabrics, especially those in her favorite color, red. While toile is all the rage, Tammy wants to redecorate a room in her house with its happy theme. With this striking composition, she's off to an excellent start!

Les Femmes Rouge

Made by Velda Grubbs
Finished Block Size: 12" x 12" (31 cm x 31 cm)
Finished Quilt Size: 91" x 103" (231 cm x 262 cm)

Yardage Requirements

Yardage is based on 45"w fabric.

- ☐ 1³/₄ yds (1.6 m) of cream print
- ■ 1⁷/₈ yds (1.7 m) of red print No. 1
- ■ 1¹/₄ yds (1.1 m) of red print No. 2
- ☐ 5 yds (4.6 m) of red toile print*
  - ³/₄ yds (69 cm) of binding fabric
  - 9 yds (8.2 m) of backing fabric
  - 120" x 120" (3.0 m x 3.0 m) batting
  - * An extra 2 yards has been added for the directional toile print.

Cutting out the Pieces

*All measurements include a ¹/₄" seam allowance. Follow **Rotary Cutting**, page 49, to cut fabric.*

From cream print: ☐
- Cut 8 crosswise strips (A) 2¹/₂" x 42" for strip sets.
- Cut 8 crosswise strips (B) 4¹/₂" x 42" for inner borders.

From red print No. 1: 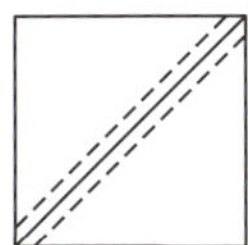
- Cut 4 strips 4⁷/₈" wide. From these strips, cut 30 squares (C) 4⁷/₈" x 4⁷/₈".
- Cut 16 crosswise strips 2¹/₂" x 42": 8 strips (D) for strip sets and 8 strips (E) for middle borders.

From red print No. 2: 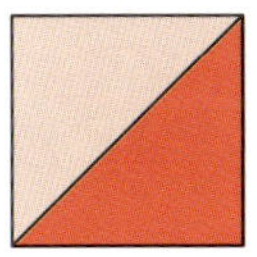
- Cut 5 strips 6⁷/₈" wide. From these strips, cut 30 squares 6⁷/₈" x 6⁷/₈". Cut each square once diagonally to make 60 triangles (F).

From red toile print: ☐
- Cut 2 strips 4¹/₂" wide. From these strips, cut 15 squares (G) 4¹/₂" x 4¹/₂" for Block A center.
- Cut 4 strips 4⁷/₈" wide. From these strips, cut 30 squares (H) 4⁷/₈" x 4⁷/₈".
- Cut 2 lengthwise strips (I) 9¹/₂" x 84¹/₂" for outer side borders.
- Cut 5 crosswise strips (J) 9¹/₂" x 42" for outer top and bottom borders.
- Cut 15 squares on point (K) 9" x 9", centering a scene on each square.

From binding fabric:
- Cut 10 strips 2¹/₂"w.

Making the Blocks

*Follow **Piecing and Pressing**, page 51, to make the quilt top.*

Block A

1. Draw a diagonal line (corner to corner) on wrong side of each of 30 toile print squares (H). With right sides together, place a toile square on top of a No. 1 red print square (C). Stitch seam ¹/₄" from each side of drawn line (**Fig. 1**).

Fig. 1

2. Trim along drawn line and press open to make 2 **Unit 1** triangle-squares. Make 60 **Unit 1's**.

Unit 1
(make 60)

3. Sew a cream print strip (A) to a No. 1 red print strip (D) as shown to make **Strip Set A**. Make 8 **Strip Set A's**.

Strip Set A
(make 8)

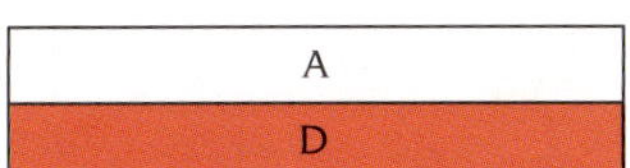

4. Cut across **Strip Set A's** at 4¹/₂" intervals to make **Unit 2**. Make 60 **Unit 2's**.

Unit 2
(make 60)

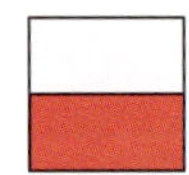

5. Sew 2 **Unit 1's** and **Unit 2** together to make **Unit 3**. Make 30 **Unit 3's**.

Unit 3
(make 30)

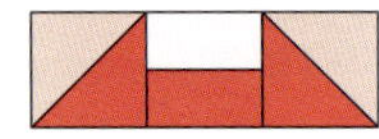

6. Sew 2 **Unit 2's** to a toile square (G) to make **Unit 4**. Make 15 **Unit 4's**.

Unit 4
(make 15)

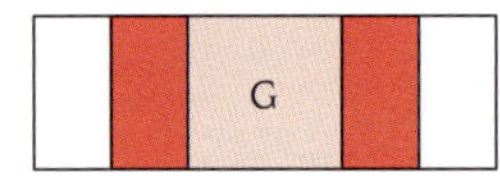

7. Sew 2 **Unit 3's** to a **Unit 4** as shown to make **Block A**. Make 15 **Block A's**.

Block A Diagram
(make 15)

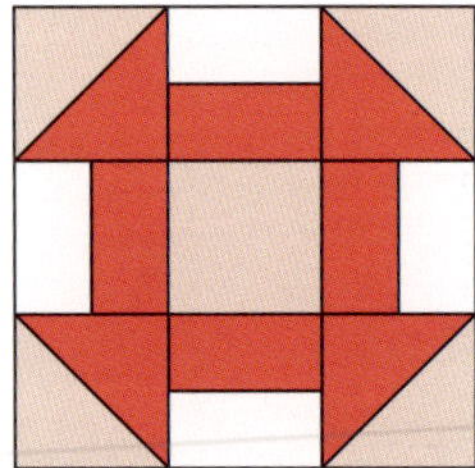

Block B
1. Sew 4 No. 2 red print triangles (F) to a toile square (K) as shown to make **Block B**. Make 15 **Block B's**.

Block B Diagram
(make 15)

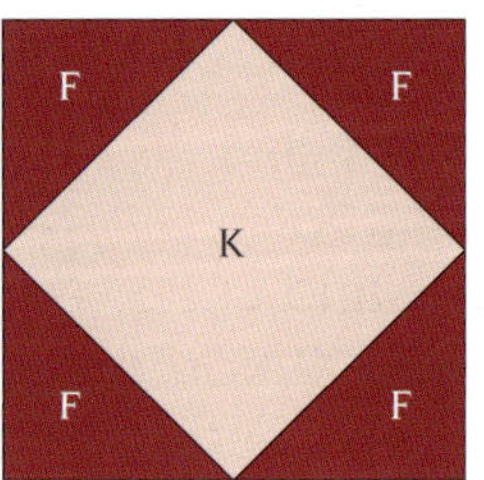

Assembling the Quilt Top

*Follow **Piecing and Pressing**, page 51, to make the quilt top. Refer to photo, page 18, and **Quilt Top Diagram** for placement.*

1. Sew 3 **Block A's** and 2 **Block B's** together as shown to make **Unit 5**. Make 3 **Unit 5's**.

Unit 5
(make 3)

2. Sew 3 **Block B's** and 2 **Block A's** together as shown to make **Unit 6**. Make 3 **Unit 6's**.

Unit 6
(make 3)

3. Sew **Unit 5's** and **Unit 6's** together as shown to make Quilt Top Center**.**

Adding the Borders

*Follow **Piecing and Pressing**, page 51, and **Adding Squared Borders**, page 54, to add borders to Quilt Top Center.*

1. Measure across the center of the quilt top to determine the length of side borders. Sew 2 cream border strips (B) together and cut to the determined measurement. Make 2 side borders and sew to sides of Quilt Top Center.
2. Measure across the center of the quilt top, including attached borders, to determine the length of top and bottom borders. Sew 2 cream border strips (B) together and cut to the determined measurement. Make 2 borders and sew to top and bottom of Quilt Top Center.
3. Repeat **Steps 1** and **2** above to make and attach No. 1 red print middle border strips (E) to pieced quilt top.
4. Sew outer side border strips (I) to pieced quilt top. Repeat **Step 2** above to make and attach toile print outer top and bottom border strips (J) to quilt.

Completing the Quilt

1. Follow **Quilting**, page 54, to mark, layer, and quilt as desired. Our quilt was machine quilted.
2. Follow **Making Straight Grain Binding**, page 58, to make $11\frac{1}{8}$ yds of $2\frac{1}{2}$"w binding.
3. Follow **Attaching Binding with Mitered Corners**, page 58, to attach binding to quilt.

Quilt Top Diagram

Liver Snaps

When a pretty quilt has such an odd name, you have to ask about it. Tammy's oldest daughter is named Olivia, but her nickname is Liver Snaps. Olivia loves blue and yellow together, but Tammy says a more appropriate color combination may be tans and purples for the peanut butter and jelly sandwiches that Olivia took to kindergarten every day! Perhaps there's a future quilt in there somewhere ...

Liver Snaps

Made by Velda Grubbs
Finished Block Size: 12" x 12" (31 cm x 31 cm)
Finished Quilt Size excluding Prairie Points: 60" x 72" (152 cm x 183 cm)

Yardage Requirements

Yardage is based on 45"w fabric.

☐ $^5/_8$ yd (57 cm) of white print
☐ $1^5/_8$ yds (1.5 m) of yellow print
☐ $2^1/_4$ yds (2.1 m) of floral print
☐ $^5/_8$ yd (57 cm) of light blue print
☐ $1^1/_2$ yds (1.4 m) of dark blue print
☐ $1^3/_4$ yds (1.6 m) of green print
   $4^1/_2$ yds (4.1 m) of backing fabric
   72" x 90" (1.8 m x 2.3 m) batting

Cutting out the Pieces

All measurements include a $^1/_4$" seam allowance. Follow **Rotary Cutting**, *page 49, to cut fabric.*

From white print: ☐
- Cut 8 strips $2^1/_2$" wide. From these strips, cut 48 rectangles (A) $2^1/_2$" x $4^1/_2$" and 32 squares (B) $2^1/_2$" x $2^1/_2$" for Prairie Points.

From yellow print: ☐
- Cut 2 lengthwise strips (C) $2^1/_2$" x $52^1/_2$" for inner side borders.
- Cut 2 lengthwise strips (D) $40^1/_2$" x $2^1/_2$" for inner top and bottom borders.
- From remaining width, cut 2 strips $4^1/_2$" wide. From these strips, cut 12 squares (E) $4^1/_2$" x $4^1/_2$".
- From remaining width, cut 3 strips $2^1/_2$" wide. From these strips, cut 32 squares (F) $2^1/_2$" x $2^1/_2$" for Prairie Points.

From floral print: ☐
- Cut 2 strips $2^1/_2$" wide. From these strips, cut 31 squares (G) $2^1/_2$" x $2^1/_2$" for Prairie Points.
- Cut 4 lengthwise strips (H) $6^1/_2$" x 64" for outer borders.
- From remaining width, cut 16 strips $4^1/_2$" wide. From these strips, cut 48 squares (I) $4^1/_2$" x $4^1/_2$".

From light blue print: ☐
- Cut 8 strips $2^1/_2$" wide. From these strips, cut 48 rectangles (J) $2^1/_2$" x $4^1/_2$" and 32 squares (K) $2^1/_2$" x $2^1/_2$" for Prairie Points.

From dark blue print: ☐
- Cut 2 lengthwise strips (L) $2^1/_2$" x $48^1/_2$" for side framing.

- Cut 2 lengthwise strips (M) $2^1/_2$" x $40^1/_2$" for top and bottom framing.
- From remaining width, cut 12 strips $2^1/_2$" wide. From these strips, cut 31 squares (N) $2^1/_2$" x $2^1/_2$" for Prairie Points and 104 squares (O) $2^1/_2$" x $2^1/_2$".

From green print: ☐
- Cut 2 lengthwise strips (P) $2^1/_2$" x $56^1/_2$" for middle side borders.
- Cut 2 lengthwise strips (Q) $2^1/_2$" x $44^1/_2$" for middle top and bottom borders.
- From remaining width, cut 3 strips $2^1/_2$" wide. From these strips, cut 30 squares (R) $2^1/_2$" x $2^1/_2$" for Prairie Points.

Making the Blocks

Follow **Piecing and Pressing**, *page 51, to make the blocks.*

1. Place a dark blue square (O) on a light blue rectangle (J) and stitch diagonally as shown in **Fig. 1**. Trim $^1/_4$" from stitching line; press open. Repeat with a matching square on opposite end of rectangle as shown in **Fig. 2** to make **Unit 1**. Make 48 **Unit 1's**.

Fig. 1

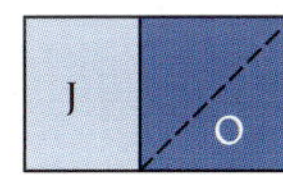

Fig. 2

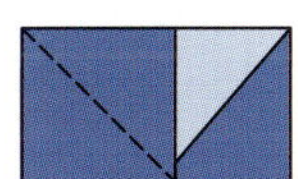

Unit 1
(make 48)

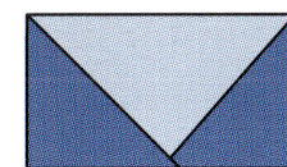

2. Sew a **Unit 1** to a white print rectangle (A) as shown to make **Unit 2**. Make 48 **Unit 2's**.

Unit 2
(make 48)

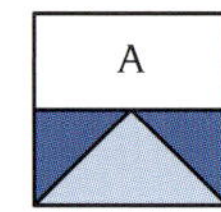

3. Sew 2 **Unit 2's** to a yellow print square (E) as shown to make **Unit 3**. Make 12 **Unit 3's**.

Unit 3
(make 12)

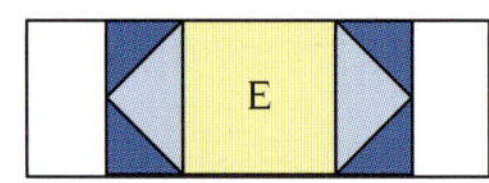

4. Sew 2 floral print squares (I) to a **Unit 2** as shown to make **Unit 4**. Make 24 **Unit 4's**.

Unit 4
(make 24)

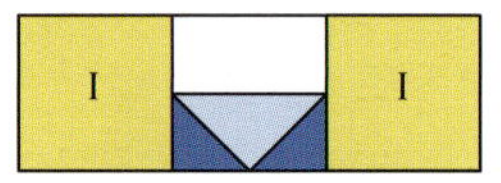

5. Sew 2 **Unit 4's** to a **Unit 3** as shown to make block. Make 12 blocks.

Block Diagram
(make 12)

Assembling the Quilt Top

*Follow **Piecing and Pressing**, page 51, to make the quilt top. Refer to photo, page 24, and **Quilt Top Diagram** for placement.*

1. Sew 3 blocks together as shown to make **Unit 5**. Make 4 **Unit 5's**.

Unit 5

2. Sew **Unit 5's** together as shown to make Quilt Top Center.

Adding the Borders

*Follow **Piecing and Pressing**, page 51, and **Adding Squared Borders**, page 54, to make the quilt top. Refer to photo, page 24, and **Quilt Top Diagram** for placement.*

1. Sew dark blue side framing strips (L), then dark blue top and bottom framing strips (M) to Quilt Top Center to make **Unit 6**.
2. Sew yellow print inner side borders (C) to **Unit 6**. Sew a dark blue square (O) to each end of the yellow print inner top and bottom borders (D). Sew borders to top and bottom of **Unit 6** to make **Unit 7**.
3. Sew green print middle side borders (P) to **Unit 7**. Sew a dark blue square (O) to each end of the green print middle top and bottom borders (Q). Sew borders to top and bottom of **Unit 7** to make **Unit 8**.
4. Measure across the center of the quilt top, including attached borders, to determine the length of outer side border strips. Cut 2 floral print strips (H) to the determined measurement and sew to sides of **Unit 8**.
5. Repeat Step 4 to cut and sew 2 floral print outer top and bottom borders to **Unit 8** to make quilt.

Completing the Quilt

1. Follow **Quilting**, page 54, to mark, layer, and quilt as desired, leaving a $^1/_2$" unquilted along the edges to attach Prairie Points. Our quilt was machine quilted.
2. For Prairie Points, fold each $2^1/_2$" square (B, F, G, K, N, and R) once diagonally and press. Fold diagonally again and press. Make 188 Prairie Points (42 each for the top and bottom edges and 52 each for the side edges) from assorted prints.

3. With raw edges even, arrange the points along each edge of quilt top, inserting the folded edge of one point into the fold opening of the next point as shown in **Fig. 3**. Pin in place.

4. Being careful not to catch the backing fabric, sew the points in place.

5. Turn points to outside of quilt top. Turn backing fabric $1/2$" to wrong side and blind stitch in place.

Fig. 3

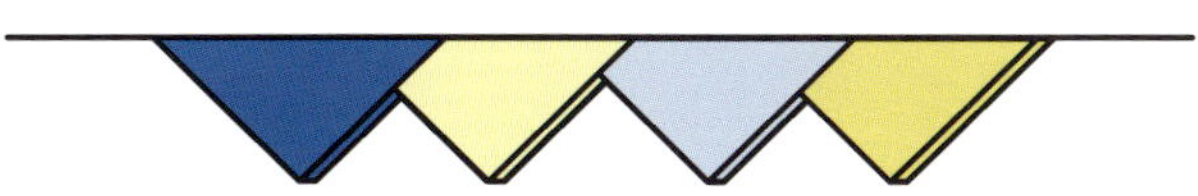

Quilt Top Diagram

Positively Posies

This large quilt borrows
two popular blocks from
Tammy's original Sunday
Sampler quilt. Floral-print
fabrics for the sashing,
binding, and appliqués are
good choices to complement
the brown-and-tan baskets.
You may wish to buy a little
extra fabric to make
matching posy or basket
pillows once your quilt
is complete.

Yardage Requirements

Yardage is based on 45"w fabric.
  5¹/₂ yds (5.0 m) of cream solid
  ⁷/₈ yd (80 cm) of dark brown print
  ¹/₄ yd (23 cm) of light brown print
  2¹/₈ yds (1.9 m) of floral print
  1¹/₄ yds (1.1 m) of dark green print
  ⁷/₈ yd (80 cm) of light green print
  ¹/₄ yd (23 cm) **each** of assorted dark yellow, dark pink, dark blue, and dark purple prints
  ¹/₄ yd (23 cm) **each** of assorted light yellow, light pink, light blue, and light purple prints
  ³/₈ yd (34 cm) of gold print for flower centers
  ³/₄ yd (69 cm) of binding fabric
  7¹/₄ yds (6.6 m) of backing fabric
  90" x 108" (2.3 m x 2.7 m) batting

Cutting out the Blocks and Borders

*All measurements include a ¹/₄" seam allowance. Follow **Rotary Cutting**, page 49, and **Adding Squared Borders**, page 54, to cut fabric.*

From cream solid:
- Cut 4 strips 12¹/₂" wide. From these strips, cut 10 squares (No. 1) 12¹/₂" x 12¹/₂" for background blocks.
- Cut 2 strips 12⁷/₈" wide. From these strips, cut 5 squares 12⁷/₈" x 12⁷/₈". Cut each square once diagonally to make 10 triangles (No. 2).
- Cut 2 strips 2⁷/₈" wide. From these strips, cut 20 squares 2⁷/₈" x 2⁷/₈". Cut each square once diagonally to make 40 triangles (No. 3).
- Cut 5 strips 2¹/₂" wide. From these strips, cut 20 rectangles (No. 4) 2¹/₂" x 6¹/₂" and 10 squares (No. 5) 2¹/₂" x 2¹/₂".
- Cut 2 lengthwise strips (No. 6) 10¹/₂" x 72¹/₂" for outer side borders.
- Cut 2 lengthwise strips (No. 7) 10¹/₂" x 78¹/₂" for outer top and bottom borders.

From dark brown print:
- Cut 4 strips 2⁷/₈" wide. From these strips, cut 55 squares 2⁷/₈" x 2⁷/₈". Cut each square once diagonally to make 110 triangles (No. 8).

From light brown print:
- Cut 2 strips 2⁷/₈" wide. From these strips, cut 25 squares 2⁷/₈" x 2⁷/₈". Cut each square once diagonally to make 50 triangles (No. 10).

- Cut 1 strip 2¹/₂" wide. From this strip, cut 10 squares (No. 11) 2¹/₂" x 2¹/₂".

From floral print:
- Cut 1 strip 12¹/₂" wide. Cut 15 lengthwise sashing strips (No. 12) 2¹/₂" x 12¹/₂".
- Cut 4 lengthwise sashing strips (No. 13) 2¹/₂" x 54¹/₂".
- Cut 2 lengthwise strips (No. 14) 2¹/₂" x 68¹/₂" for inner side borders.
- Cut 2 lengthwise strips (No. 15) 2¹/₂" x 58¹/₂" for top and bottom borders.

From binding fabric:
- Cut 9 strips 2¹/₂"w.

Cutting the Appliqués

*Refer to **Making Templates**, page 52, to use patterns, page 35, to make templates. **Note:** Appliqué patterns provided do not include seam allowances. Measurements given for bias strips include a ¹/₄" seam allowance. To help keep blocks organized, lay out all appliqué pieces with corresponding backgrounds as you cut.*

From dark brown print:
- Cut 10 bias strips 1¹/₂" x 15" for basket handles (A).

From light green print:
- Cut 14 yds of 1¹/₄"w continuous bias strip for stems and vines.

From dark green print:
- Cut 56 large leaves (B).
- Cut 26 small leaves; cut 26 small leaves in reverse (C).

From assorted dark yellow, dark pink, dark blue, and dark purple prints:
- Cut 14 large flowers (D).
- Cut 12 small flowers (E).

From assorted light yellow, light pink, light blue, and light purple prints:
- Cut 26 small flowers (E).

From gold print:
- Cut 38 circles (F) for flower centers.

Making the Blocks

Follow **Piecing and Pressing**, *page 51, and* **Machine Appliqué**, *page 52, to make the blocks. Refer to photo, page 30, and* **Quilt Top Diagram**, *page 34, for placement.*

Block A

1. Matching wrong sides and long edges, press dark brown strip (A) in half. Position each end of strip, with raw edges facing out, 6" from outer corners of a No. 2 cream triangle (**Fig. 1**). Pin in place. Machine stitch ¹/₄" from raw edges.

Fig. 1

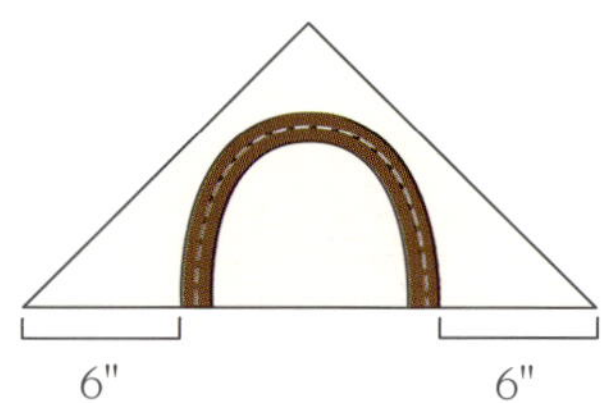

2. Press strip up and appliqué in place to make **Unit 1**. Make 10 **Unit 1's**.

Unit 1
(make 10)

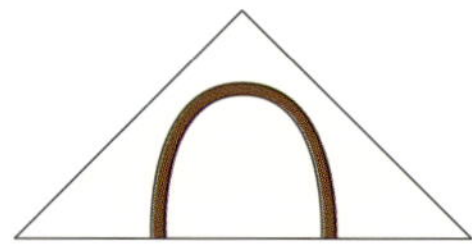

3. Sew a No. 8 dark brown triangle and a No. 10 light brown triangle together as shown to make **Unit 2**. Make 50 **Unit 2's**.

Unit 2
(make 50)

4. Sew a No. 3 cream triangle and a No. 8 dark brown triangle together as shown to make **Unit 3**. Make 20 **Unit 3's**.

Unit 3
(make 20)

5. Sew 2 No. 8 dark brown triangles and a **Unit 2** together as shown to make **Unit 4**. Make 10 **Unit 4's**.

Unit 4
(make 10)

6. Sew 2 **Unit 2's** and a No. 8 dark brown triangle together as shown to make **Unit 5**. Make 20 **Unit 5's**.

Unit 5
(make 20)

7. Sew a No. 11 light brown square and a **Unit 5** together as shown to make **Unit 6**. Make 10 **Unit 6's**.

Unit 6
(make 10)

8. Sew **Units 4, 5,** and **6** together as shown to make **Unit 7**. Make 10 **Unit 7's**.

Unit 7
(make 10)

9. Sew a No. 3 cream triangle, a No. 4 cream rectangle, and a **Unit 3** together as shown to make **Unit 8**. Make 10 **Unit 8's**.

Unit 8
(make 10)

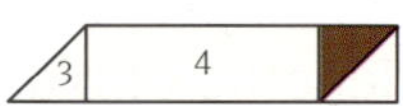

10. Sew a No. 3 cream triangle, a No. 4 cream rectangle, a **Unit 3**, and a No. 5 cream square together as shown to make **Unit 9**. Make 10 **Unit 9**'s.

Unit 9
(make 10)

11. Sew **Units 7**, **8**, and **9** together as shown to make **Unit 10**. Make 10 **Unit 10**'s.

Unit 10
(make 10)

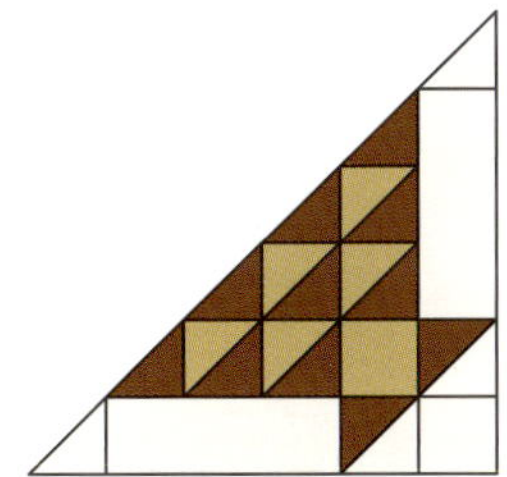

12. Sew **Units 1** and **10** together as shown to make **Block A**. Make 10 **Block A**'s.

Block A Diagram
(make 10)

Block B

1. Matching wrong sides and long edges, fold light green print continuous bias strip in half lengthwise. Do not press. Stitch $1/4$" from raw edges and trim seam allowances to $1/8$". With seam centered in back, press flat. For each block, cut four 5" lengths of bias strip for stems. The remaining bias strip will be used for the border vines.

2. To make yo-yo flower centers, turn edge of flower center (F) $1/4$" to wrong side and sew a running stitch all around edge using 2 strands of thread (**Fig. 2**). Pull threads tight from both ends and tie a knot; clip threads (**Fig. 3**). Make 38 yo-yo flower centers.

Fig. 2

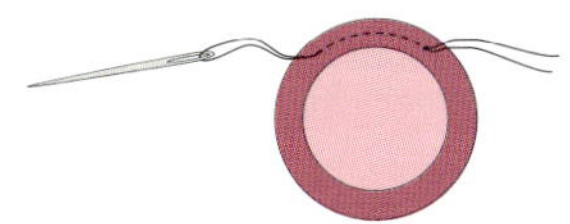

Fig. 3

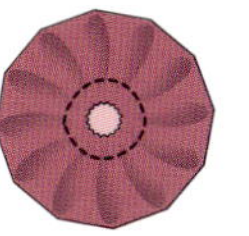

3. Position and pin in place 4 stems, 4 large leaves (B), a large flower (D), a small flower (E), and a yo- yo flower center (F) on a No. 1 cream background block as shown. Appliqué pieces in place to make **Block B**. Make 10 **Block B**'s.

Block B Diagram
(make 10)

Assembling the Quilt Top

Follow **Piecing and Pressing**, *page 51,* **Adding Squared Borders**, *page 54, and* **Machine Appliqué**, *page 52 to make the quilt top. Refer to photo, page 30, and* **Quilt Top Diagram**, *page 34, for placement.* **Note:** *Trim each block to measure* $12^{1}/_{2}$" *x* $12^{1}/_{2}$" *before adding sashing strips.*

1. Sew 2 **Block A**'s, 2 **Block B**'s, and 3 No. 12 sashing strips together as shown to make **Unit 11**. Make 3 **Unit 11**'s.

Unit 11
(make 3)

2. Sew 2 **Block A's**, 2 **Block B's**, and 3 No. 12 sashing strips together as shown to make **Unit 12**. Make 2 **Unit 12's**.

Unit 12
(make 2)

3. Sew 4 No. 13 sashing strips, 3 **Unit 11's**, and 2 **Unit 12's** together to make Quilt Top Center.
4. Sew No. 14 inner side borders, then No. 15 inner top and bottom borders to Quilt Top Center.

5. Sew No. 6 outer side borders, then No. 7 outer top and bottom borders to Quilt Top Center to make quilt top.
6. Appliqué the vines, leaves, and flowers to the outer borders.

Completing the Quilt
1. Follow **Quilting**, page 54, to mark, layer, and quilt as desired. Our quilt was machine quilted.
2. Follow **Making Straight Grain Binding**, page 58, to make 9⅞ yds of 2½"w binding.
3. Follow **Attaching Binding with Mitered Corners**, page 58, to attach binding to quilt.

Quilt Top Diagram

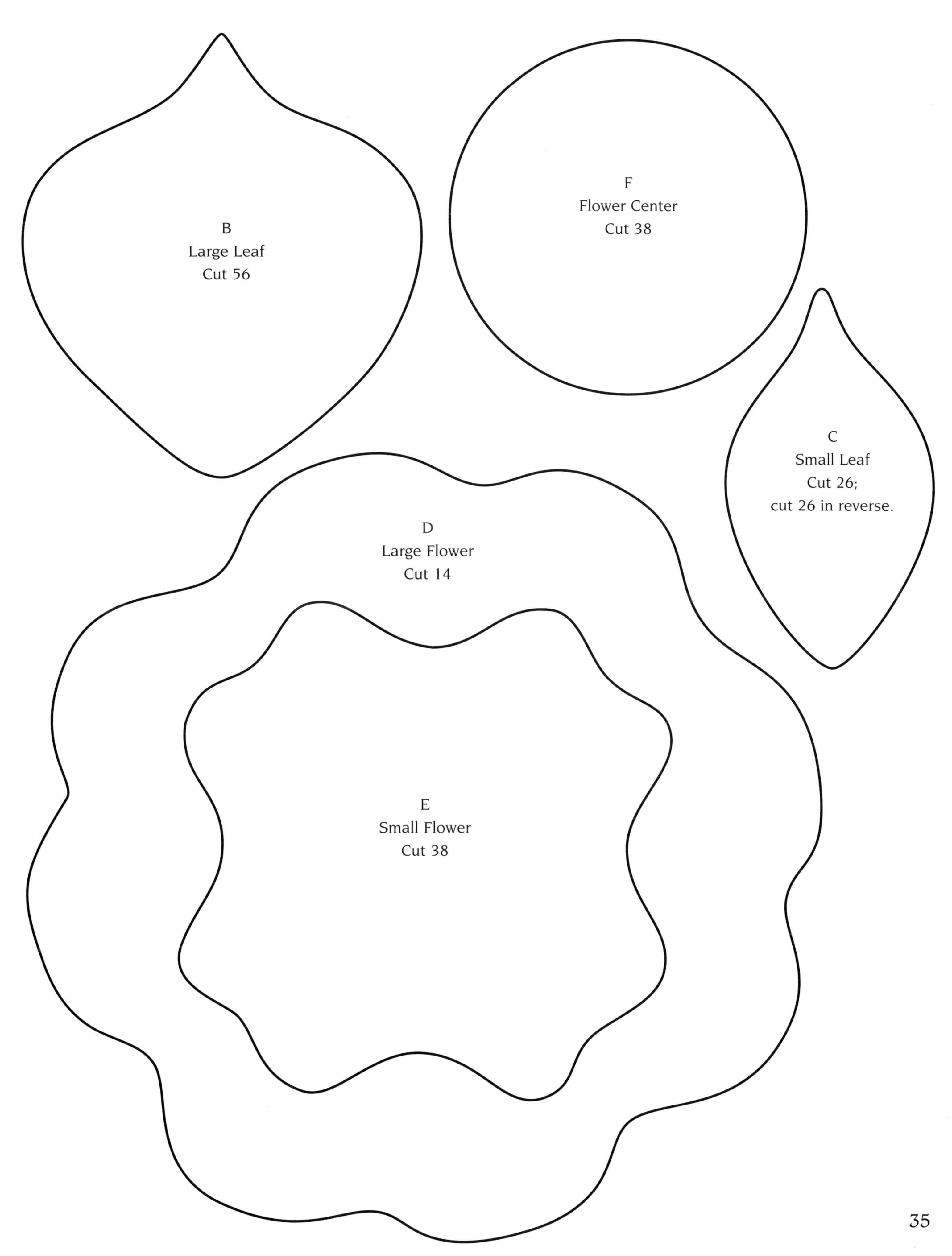

B
Large Leaf
Cut 56

F
Flower Center
Cut 38

C
Small Leaf
Cut 26;
cut 26 in reverse.

D
Large Flower
Cut 14

E
Small Flower
Cut 38

Heritage

When Tammy's nephew Trever joined the United States Air Force, his grandmother made him a quilt. This quilt is a re-creation of that first quilt, with Americana fabrics substituted for the original blues, tans, and greens. Tammy encourages us all to make this quilt for a loved one.

Heritage

Made by Velda Grubbs
Finished Block Size: 12" x 12" (31 cm x 31 cm)
Finished Quilt Size: 81" x 105" (206 cm x 267 cm)

Yardage Requirements

Yardage is based on 45"w fabric.

- ☐ 3³/₄ yds (3.4 m) of beige print
- ■ 3¹/₈ yds (2.8 m) of dark red print
- ■ ³/₄ yd (69 cm) of red stripe
- ■ ³/₄ yd (69 cm) of light blue print
- ■ 2⁵/₈ yds (2.4 m) of dark blue print
- ³/₄ yd (69 cm) of binding fabric
- 7¹/₂ yds (6.8 m) of backing fabric
- 90" x 108" (2.3 m x 2.7 m) batting

Cutting out the Pieces

*Refer to **Making Templates**, page 52, to make template using pattern, page 48. All measurements include a ¹/₄" seam allowance. Follow **Rotary Cutting**, page 49, and **Adding Squared Borders**, page 54, to cut fabric.*

From beige print: ☐

- Cut 2 lengthwise strips (A) 6¹/₂" x 88¹/₂" for middle side borders.
- Cut 2 lengthwise strips (B) 6¹/₂" x 76¹/₂" for middle top and bottom borders.
- From remaining width, cut 24 strips 2¹/₂" wide. From these strips, cut 140 squares (C) 2¹/₂" x 2¹/₂".
- Cut 7 strips 3³/₄" wide. From these strips, cut 72 squares 3³/₄" x 3³/₄". Cut each square once diagonally to make 144 triangles (D).
- Cut 3 strips 4⁷/₈" wide. From these strips, cut 18 squares 4⁷/₈" x 4⁷/₈". Cut each square once diagonally to make 36 triangles (E).

From dark red print: ■

- Cut 2 lengthwise strips (F) 2¹/₂" x 100¹/₂" for outer side borders.
- Cut 2 lengthwise strips (G) 2¹/₂" x 76¹/₂" for outer top and bottom borders.
- From remaining width:
- Cut 4 strips 2⁷/₈" wide. From these strips, cut 36 squares 2⁷/₈" x 2⁷/₈". Cut each square once diagonally to make 72 triangles (H).
- Cut 5 strips 3³/₄" wide. From these strips, cut 36 squares 3³/₄" x 3³/₄". Cut each square once diagonally to make 72 triangles (I).
- Cut 3 strips 4⁷/₈" wide. From these strips, cut 18 squares 4⁷/₈" x 4⁷/₈". Cut each square once diagonally to make 36 triangles (J).
- Cut 10 strips 2¹/₂" wide. From these strips, cut 68 rectangles (K) 2¹/₂" x 4¹/₂".

From red stripe: ■

- Cut 9 strips 2¹/₂" wide. From these strips, cut 68 rectangles (L) 2¹/₂" x 4¹/₂" and 4 squares (M) 2¹/₂" x 2¹/₂".

From light blue print: ■

- Cut 9 strips 2¹/₂" wide. From these strips, cut 68 rectangles (N) 2¹/₂" x 4¹/₂" and 4 squares (O) 2¹/₂" x 2¹/₂".

From dark blue print: ■

- Cut 2 lengthwise strips (P) 2¹/₂" x 84¹/₂" for inner side borders.
- Cut 2 lengthwise strips (Q) 2¹/₂" x 60¹/₂" for inner top and bottom borders.
- From remaining width, cut 10 strips 2¹/₂" wide. From these strips, cut 68 rectangles (R) 2¹/₂" x 4¹/₂".
- Use Template S, page 48, to cut 72 pieces (S).

From binding fabric:

- Cut 10 strips 2¹/₂"w.

Making the Blocks

*Follow **Piecing and Pressing**, page 51, to make the blocks.*

Block A

1. Sew a beige print square (C), a dark red print triangle (H), and a beige print triangle (D) together as shown to make **Unit 1**. Make 72 **Unit 1**'s.

Unit 1 (make 72)

2. Sew a beige print triangle (D) and a dark red print triangle (I) together as shown to make **Unit 2**. Make 72 **Unit 2**'s.

Unit 2 (make 72)

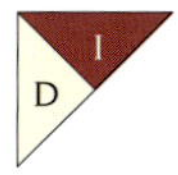

3. Sew a **Unit 1** to a **Unit 2** as shown to make **Unit 3**. Make 72 **Unit 3**'s.

Unit 3 (make 72)

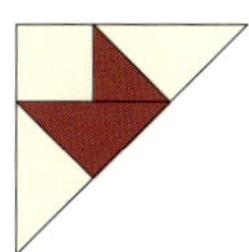

4. Sew piece (S) to a **Unit 3** as shown to make **Unit 4**. Make 72 **Unit 4's**.

Unit 4 (make 72)

5. Sew a beige print triangle (E) to **Unit 4** as shown to make **Unit 5**. Make 36 **Unit 5's**.

Unit 5 (make 36)

6. Sew a dark red print triangle (J) to **Unit 4** as shown to make **Unit 6**. Make 36 **Unit 6's**.

Unit 6 (make 36)

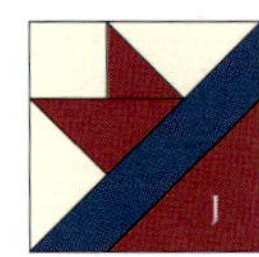

7. Sew 2 **Unit 5's** and 2 **Unit 6's** together as shown to make **Block A**. Make 18 **Block A's**.

Block A Diagram (make 18)

Block B

1. To sew dark blue print rectangle (R) to beige print square (C), mark a dot $1/4$" in from one corner of the square. With right sides together, stitch the seam from the outer edge to the dot, backstitching at dot as shown in **Fig. 1**. Press open.

Fig. 1

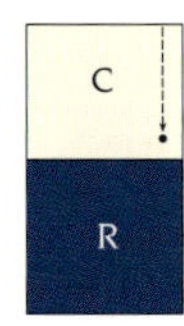

2. Sew red stripe rectangle (L) and light blue print rectangle (N) to square as shown in **Fig. 2**.

Fig. 2

3. To sew dark red print rectangle (K) to block, mark a dot $1/4$" in from one corner of rectangle. With right sides together, match dot on rectangle to dot on square. Sew rectangle from outer edge to dot, backstitching at dot (**Fig. 3**). Press open.

Fig. 3

4. To complete the square, fold dark blue print rectangle (R) back over square and dark red print rectangle (K). Matching raw edges, complete the first seam to make **Unit 7**. Repeat Steps 1-4 to make 34 **Unit 7's**.

Unit 7
(make 34)

5. Repeat **Steps 1-4** using alternate color placement as shown to make **Unit 8**. Make 34 **Unit 8's**.

Unit 8
(make 34)

6. Sew 2 **Unit 7's** and 2 **Unit 8's** together as shown to make **Block B**. Make 17 **Block B's**.

Block B Diagram (make 17)

Assembling the Quilt Top

*Follow **Piecing and Pressing**, page 51, to make the quilt top. Refer to photo, page 38, and **Quilt Top Diagram** for placement.*

1. Sew 3 **Block A's** and 2 **Block B's** together to make **Unit 9**. Make 4 **Unit 9's**.
2. Sew 3 **Block B's** and 2 **Block A's** together to make **Unit 10**. Make 3 **Unit 10's**.
3. Sew **Unit 9's** and **Unit 10's** together to make Quilt Top Center.

Adding the Borders

*Follow **Piecing and Pressing**, page 51, and **Adding Squared Borders**, page 54, to add the borders. Refer to photo, page 38, and **Quilt Top Diagram** for placement.*

1. Sew dark blue print inner side borders (P) to Quilt Top Center. Sew a red stripe square (M) to each end of the dark blue print inner top and bottom borders (Q). Sew borders to top and bottom of Quilt Top Center.
2. Sew beige print middle side borders (A), then beige print middle top and bottom borders (B) to pieced center.
3. Sew dark red print outer side borders (F) to pieced center. Sew a light blue print square (O) to each end of the dark red print outer top and bottom borders (G). Sew borders to top and bottom of pieced center to make quilt top.

Completing the Quilt

1. Follow **Quilting**, page 54, to mark, layer, and quilt as desired. Our quilt was machine quilted using gold metallic thread.
2. Follow **Making Straight Grain Binding**, page 58, to make $10^5/_8$ yds of $2^1/_2$"w binding.
3. Follow **Attaching Binding with Mitered Corners**, page 58, to attach binding to quilt.

Quilt Top Diagram

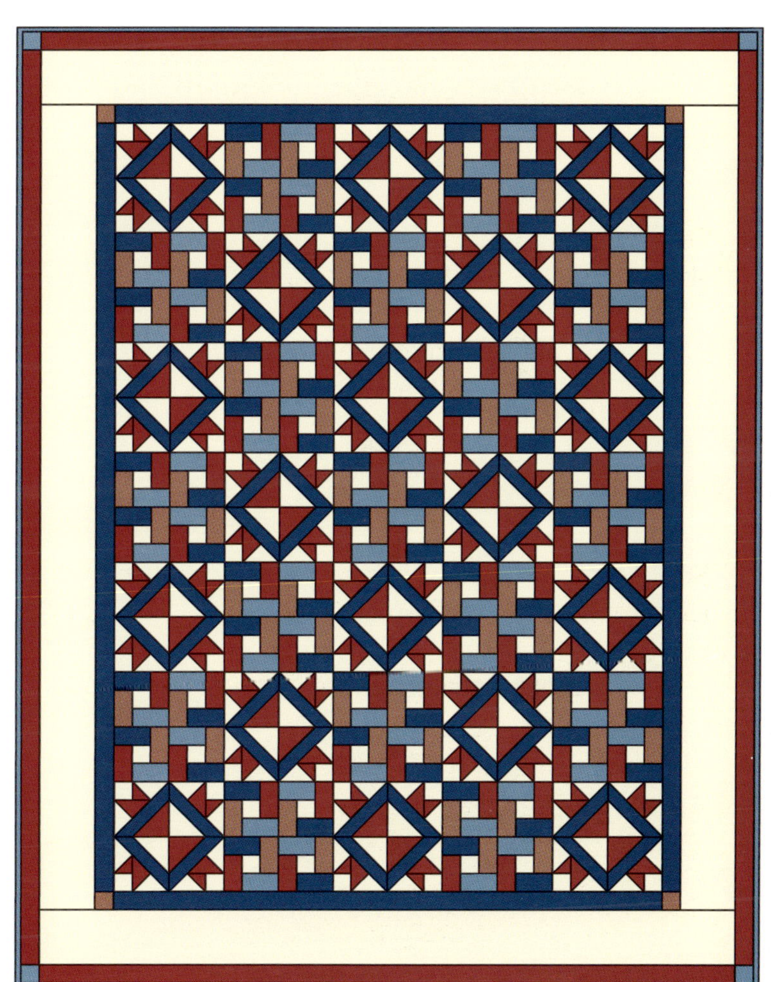

Not-So-Square Granny

When Tammy inherited a 1960's-style granny-square afghan, she couldn't resist making a quilt based on the familiar crochet pattern. The bright colors are like those found in the popular afghan, and Tammy says the paper-pieced blocks are just as fun to make as they appear to be. We're sure you know someone who would dig this psychedelic lap quilt for their retro décor!

Not-So-Square Granny

Made by Velda Grubbs
Finished Block Size: 12" x 12" (31 cm x 31 cm)
Finished Quilt Size: 53" x 67" (135 cm x 170 cm)

Yardage Requirements

Yardage is based on 45"w fabric.

- ■ 3³/₄ yds (3.4 m) of black solid
- ◩ ³/₈ yd (34 cm) **each** of 16 assorted prints
- ³/₄ yd (69 cm) of binding fabric
- 3¹/₂ yds (3.2 m) of backing fabric
- 72" x 90" (1.8 m x 2.3 m) batting

Cutting out the Pieces

Follow **Rotary Cutting***, page 49, and* **Adding Squared Borders***, page 54, to cut fabric. All measurements include a ¹/₄" seam allowance.*

From black solid: ■

- Cut 2 lengthwise strips (A) 2¹/₂" x 62¹/₂" for outer side borders.
- Cut 2 lengthwise strips (B) 2¹/₂" x 52¹/₂" for outer top and bottom borders.
- Cut 2 lengthwise strips (C) 4¹/₂" x 54¹/₂" for inner side borders.
- Cut 2 lengthwise strips (D) 4¹/₂" x 48¹/₂" for inner top and bottom borders.
- Cut 3 lengthwise strips (E) 2¹/₂" x 40¹/₂" for sashings.
- Cut 8 lengthwise strips (F) 2¹/₂" x 12¹/₂" for sashings.
- Cut 240 rectangles (G) 1¹/₂" x 3" for foundation pieces Nos. 2, 4, 7, 9, and 16.
- Cut 192 rectangles (H) 2" x 3" for foundation pieces Nos. 5, 10, 12, and 14.

From assorted prints: ◩

- Cut 48 rectangles (I) 2¹/₂" x 3" for foundation piece No. 1 (4 of the same color for each block).
- Cut 96 rectangles (J) 2¹/₂" x 3" for foundation pieces Nos. 3 and 6 (8 of the same color for each block).
- Cut 192 rectangles (K) 2¹/₂" x 3" for foundation pieces Nos. 8, 11, 13, and 15 (16 of the same color for each block).
- Cut 48 squares (L) 2¹/₂" x 2¹/₂" for middle corners (4 of the same color for each block).
- Cut 48 squares (M) 2¹/₂" x 2¹/₂" for outer corners (4 of the same color for each block).
- Cut 72 squares (N) 4¹/₂" x 4¹/₂" for Prairie Points (5 each of 8 different prints and 4 each of remaining prints).

Making the Blocks

Follow **Piecing and Pressing***, page 51, to make the blocks. Refer to photo, page 44, and* **Quilt Top Diagram***, page 47, for placement.*

Paper Piecing the Block

To prepare your sewing machine for foundation piecing, insert a 90/14 needle. This needle will help perforate your paper to make the needle-punch foundations. This needle should then be reserved exclusively for the use of foundation work, as paper will dull needles quickly. Set your machine to a short straight stitch (18 stitches per inch). It is helpful to use an open-toe presser foot.

1. Using a fine-point marker and leaving at least a 1" space on all sides of each pattern, trace solid and dashed lines of Foundation Patterns Nos. 1 - 3, page 48.

2. To make needle-punch foundations, place up to eight pieces of foundation paper (notebook paper will do) under traced pattern and secure with pins. With your needle in your machine but no thread, sew precisely on the solid lines. The punched holes serve as your sewing guide. Trim each punched pattern leaving at least 1" around pattern.

3. For **each** block, make 4 punched patterns of each Foundation Pattern Nos.1 - 3.

4. With wrong sides together, completely cover area 1 of Foundation Pattern No. 1 with a print rectangle (I). Pin or glue fabric (using a small dab from a glue stick) in place (**Fig. 1**). Fold foundation on line between area 1 and area 2. Trim fabric ¹/₄" from fold (**Fig. 2**). Unfold foundation.

Fig. 1

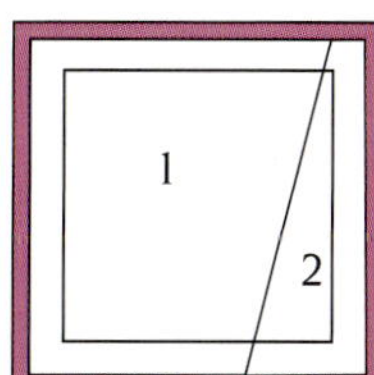

Fig. 2

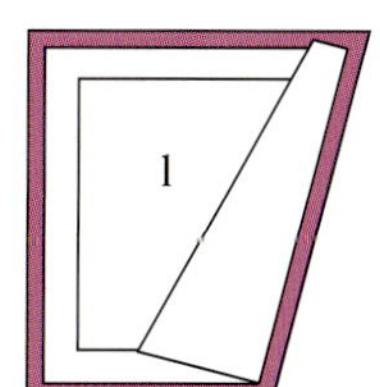

5. Matching trimmed edges, place black rectangle (G) on print rectangle, right sides together, making sure fabric extends beyond outer edges of area 2. Turn foundation over to front and pin. Sew along punched line between areas 1 and 2 (blue lines on pattern), extending sewing a few stitches beyond beginning and ending of line (**Fig. 3**).

Fig. 3

6. Open out black rectangle; press. Trim fabric and foundation $^1/_4$" from edge of block (dashed line on pattern) to make **Unit 1**. Make 4 **Unit 1**'s.

Unit 1
(make 4)

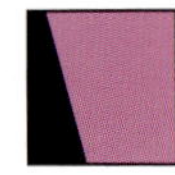

7. Sew 4 **Unit 1**'s together as shown to make **Unit 2**.

Unit 2

8. Repeat **Steps 4 - 6** for Foundation Patterns Nos. 2 and 3 using a different color print for each. Add pieces in same manner in numerical order until foundation is covered. Trim fabric and foundation $^1/_4$" outside punched lines. Make 4 each of **Units 3** and **4**.

Unit 3
(make 4)

Unit 4
(make 4)

9. Sew a **Unit 3** to 2 sides of a **Unit 2**. Sew a print square (L) to each end of a **Unit 3** to make **Unit 5**. Make 2 **Unit 5**'s. Sew 2 **Unit 5**'s to the top and bottom of **Unit 2** to make **Unit 6**.

Unit 5
(make 2)

Unit 6

10. Sew a **Unit 4** to each side of pieced center. Sew a print square (M) to each end of a **Unit 4** to make **Unit 7**. Sew **Unit 7**'s to top and bottom of block center to complete the block. Make 12 blocks.

Block Diagram
(make 12)

Assembling the Quilt Top

*Follow **Piecing and Pressing**, page 51, to make the quilt top. Refer to photo, page 44, and **Quilt Top Diagram** for placement.*

1. Sew 2 sashing strips (F) and 3 blocks together to make **Unit 8**. Make 4 **Unit 8's**.
2. Sew 3 sashing strips (E) and 4 **Unit 8's** together to make Quilt Top Center.

Adding the Borders

*Follow **Piecing and Pressing**, page 51, and **Adding Squared Borders**, page 54, to add the borders. Refer to photo, page 44, and **Quilt Top Diagram** for placement.*

1. Sew black solid inner side borders (C), then black solid inner top and bottom borders (D) to Quilt Top Center to make **Unit 9**.
2. For Prairie Points, fold a square (N) once diagonally and press. Fold diagonally again and press. Make 72 Prairie Points from assorted prints (16 each for the top and bottom borders and 20 each for the side borders).
3. With raw edges even, arrange the points along each edge of **Unit 9**, inserting the folded edge of one point into the fold opening of the next point as shown in **Fig. 4**. Pin in place.

Fig. 4

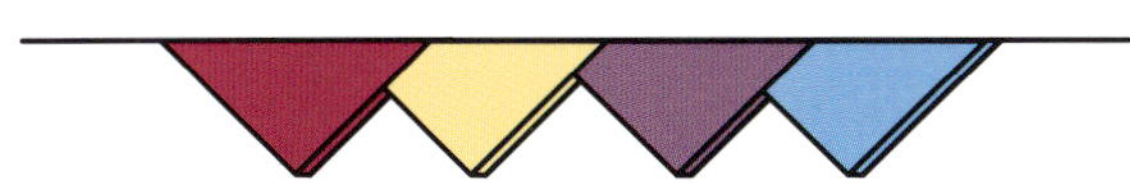

4. Using a ¹/₄" seam allowance, baste the points in place. Hand tack each point in place on the inner borders.
5. Sew black solid outer side borders (A), then black solid outer top and bottom borders (B) to **Unit 9** to make quilt.

Completing the Quilt

1. Follow **Quilting**, page 54, to mark, layer, and quilt as desired. Our quilt was machine quilted.
2. Cut a 27" square of binding fabric. Follow **Making Continuous Bias Strip Binding**, page 57, to make 7 yds of 2¹/₂"w binding.
3. Follow **Attaching Binding with Mitered Corners**, page 58, to attach binding to quilt.

Quilt Top Diagram

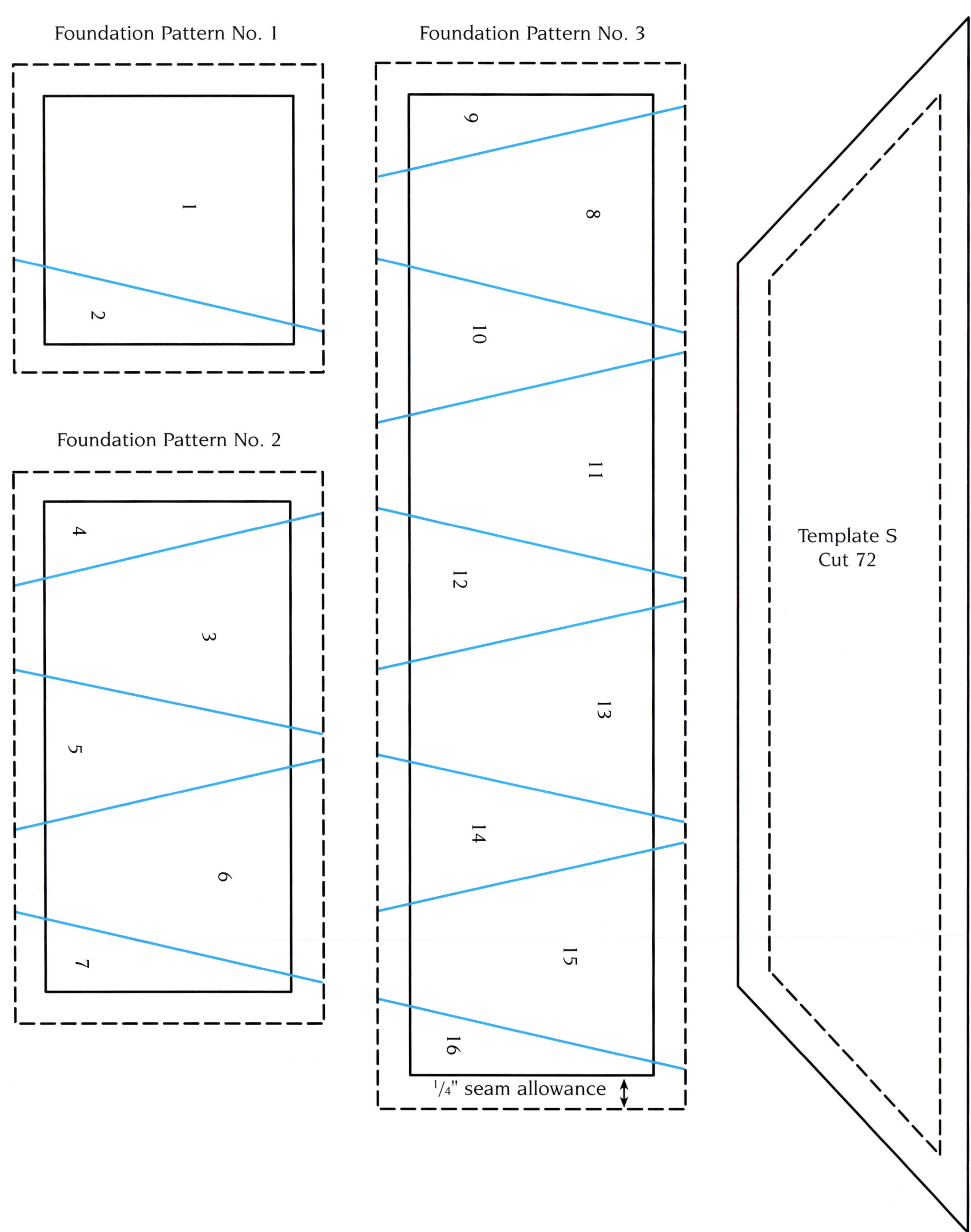

Foundation Pattern No. 1
Foundation Pattern No. 2
Foundation Pattern No. 3
Template S
Cut 72
1/4" seam allowance

GENERAL INSTRUCTIONS

Complete instructions are given for making each of the quilts shown in this book. To make your quilting easier and more enjoyable, we encourage you to carefully read all of the general instructions, study the color photographs, and familiarize yourself with the individual project instructions before beginning a project.

FABRICS

Selecting Fabrics

Choose high-quality, medium-weight 100% cotton fabrics such as broadcloth or calico. All-cotton fabrics hold a crease better, fray less, and are easier to quilt than cotton/polyester blends. All the fabrics for a quilt should be of comparable weight and weave. Check the end of the fabric bolt for fiber content and width.

The yardage requirements listed for each project are based on 45" wide fabric with a "usable" width of 42" after shrinkage and trimming selvages. Your actual usable width will probably vary slightly from fabric to fabric. Though most fabrics will yield 42" or more, if you find a fabric that you suspect will yield a narrower usable width, you will need to purchase additional yardage to compensate. Our recommended yardage lengths should be adequate for occasional re-squaring of fabric when many cuts are required, but it never hurts to buy a little more fabric for insurance against a narrower usable width, the occasional cutting error, or to have on hand for making coordinating projects.

Preparing Fabrics

All fabrics should be washed, dried, and pressed before cutting.

1. To check colorfastness before washing, cut a small piece of the fabric and place in a glass of hot water with a little detergent. Leave fabric in the water for a few minutes. Remove fabric from water and blot with white paper towels. If any color bleeds onto the towels, wash the fabric separately with warm water and detergent, then rinse until the water runs clear. If fabric continues to bleed, choose another fabric.

2. Unfold yardage and separate fabrics by color. To help reduce raveling, use scissors to snip a small triangle from each corner of your fabric pieces. Machine wash fabrics in warm water with a small amount of mild laundry detergent. Do not use fabric softener. Rinse well and then dry fabrics in the dryer, checking long fabric lengths occasionally to make sure they are not tangling.

3. To make ironing easier, remove fabrics from dryer while they are slightly damp. Refold each fabric lengthwise (as it was on the bolt) with wrong sides together and matching selvages. If necessary, adjust slightly at selvages so that fold lays flat. Press each fabric using a steam iron set on "Cotton."

ROTARY CUTTING

Based on the idea that you can easily cut strips of fabric and then cut those strips into smaller pieces, rotary cutting has brought speed and accuracy to quiltmaking. Observe safety precautions when using the rotary cutter, since it is extremely sharp. Develop a habit of retracting the blade guard just before making a cut and closing it immediately afterward, before laying down the cutter.

1. Follow **Preparing Fabrics** to wash, dry, and press fabrics.

2. Cut all strips from the selvage-to-selvage width of the fabric unless otherwise indicated in project instructions. Place fabric on the cutting mat, as shown in **Fig. 1**, page 50, with the fold of the fabric toward you. To straighten the uneven fabric edge, make the first "squaring up" cut by placing the right edge of the rotary cutting ruler over the left raw edge of the fabric. Place right-angle triangle (or another rotary cutting ruler) with the lower edge carefully aligned with the fold and the left edge against the ruler (**Fig. 1**). Hold the ruler firmly with your left hand, placing your little finger off the left edge to anchor the ruler. Remove the triangle, pick up the rotary cutter, and retract the blade guard. Using a smooth downward motion, make the cut by running the blade of the rotary cutter firmly along the right hand edge of the ruler as shown in **Fig. 2**, page 50. Always cut in a direction away from your body and immediately close the blade guard after each cut.

Fig. 1

Fig. 2

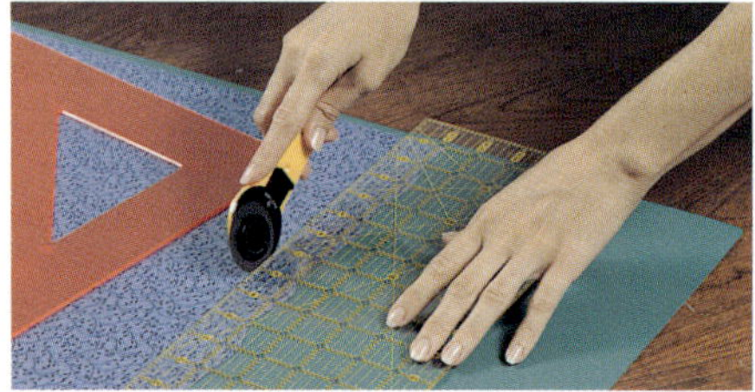

3. To cut each of the strips required for a project, place the ruler over the cut edge of the fabric, aligning desired marking on the ruler with the cut edge (**Fig. 3**); make the cut. When cutting several strips from a single piece of fabric, it is important to occasionally use the ruler and triangle to ensure that cuts are still at a perfect right angle to the fold. If not, repeat Step 2 to straighten.

Fig. 3

4. To square up selvage ends of a strip before cutting pieces, refer to **Fig. 4** and place folded strip on mat with selvage ends to your right. Aligning a horizontal marking on ruler with 1 long edge of strip, use rotary cutter to trim selvage to make end of strip square and even (**Fig. 4**). Turn strip (or entire mat) so that cut end is to your left before making subsequent cuts.

Fig. 4

5. Pieces such as rectangles and squares can now be cut from strips. Usually strips remain folded, and pieces are cut in pairs after ends of strips are squared up. To cut squares or rectangles from a strip, place ruler over left end of strip, aligning desired marking on ruler with cut end of strip. To ensure perfectly square cuts, align a horizontal marking on ruler with 1 long edge of strip (**Fig. 5**) before making the cut.

Fig. 5

6. To cut 2 triangles from a square, cut square the size indicated in the project instructions. Cut square once diagonally to make 2 triangles (**Fig. 6**).

Fig. 6

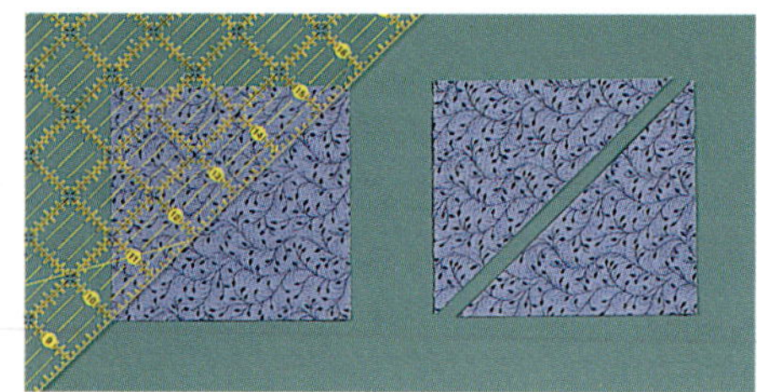

7. To cut 4 triangles from a square, cut square the size indicated in the project instructions. Cut square twice diagonally to make 4 triangles (**Fig. 7**). You may find it helpful to use a small rotary cutting mat so that the mat can be turned to make second cut without disturbing fabric pieces.

Fig. 7

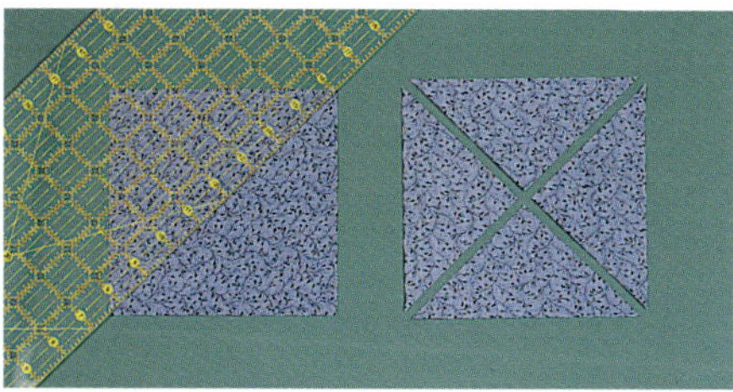

8. After some practice, you may want to try stacking up to 6 fabric layers when making cuts. When stacking strips, match long cut edges and follow Step 4 to square up ends of strip stack. Carefully turn stack (or entire mat) so that squared-up ends are to your left before making subsequent cuts. After cutting, check accuracy of pieces. Some shapes, such as diamonds, are more difficult to cut accurately in stacks.

9. In some cases, strips will be sewn together into strip sets before being cut into smaller units. When cutting a strip set, align a seam in strip set with a horizontal marking on the ruler to maintain square cuts (**Fig. 8**). We do not recommend stacking strip sets for rotary cutting.

Fig. 8

10. Most borders for quilts in this book are cut along the more stable lengthwise grain to minimize wavy edges caused by stretching. To remove selvages before cutting lengthwise strips, place fabric on mat with selvages to your left and squared-up end at bottom of mat. Placing ruler over selvage and using squared-up edge instead of fold, follow Step 2 to cut away selvages as you did raw edges (**Fig. 9**). After making a cut the length of the mat, move the next section of fabric to be cut onto the mat. Repeat until you have removed selvages from required length of fabric.

Fig. 9

11. After removing selvages, place ruler over left edge of fabric, aligning desired marking on ruler with cut edge of fabric. Make cuts as in Step 3. After each cut, move next section of fabric onto mat as in Step 10.

PIECING AND PRESSING

Precise cutting, followed by accurate piecing and careful pressing, will ensure that all the pieces of your quilt top fit together well.

Piecing

Set sewing machine stitch length for approximately 11 stitches per inch. Use a new, sharp needle suited for medium-weight woven fabric. Use a neutral-colored general-purpose sewing thread (not quilting thread) in the needle and in the bobbin. Stitch first on a scrap of fabric to check upper and bobbin thread tension; make any adjustments necessary. For good results, it is essential that you stitch with an accurate $1/4$" seam allowance. On many sewing machines, the measurement from the needle to the outer edge of the presser foot is $1/4$". If this is the case with your machine, the presser foot is your best guide. If not, measure $1/4$" from the needle and mark throat plate with a piece of masking tape. Special presser feet that are exactly $1/4$" wide are also available for most sewing machines.

When piecing, always place pieces right sides together and match raw edges; pin if necessary. (If using straight pins, remove the pins just before they reach the sewing machine needle.)

Pressing

Use a steam iron set on "Cotton" for all pressing. Press as you sew, taking care to prevent small folds along seamlines. Seam allowances are almost always pressed to one side, usually toward the darker fabric. However, to reduce bulk it may occasionally be necessary to press seam allowances toward the lighter fabric or even to press them open. In order to prevent a dark fabric seam allowance from showing through a light fabric, trim the darker seam allowance slightly narrower than the lighter seam allowance. To press long seams, such as those in long strip sets, without curving or other distortion, lay strips across the width of the ironing board.

Making Templates

Patterns for piecing templates include seam allowances; those for appliqué do not. To make a template from a pattern, use a permanent fine-point marker or pen to carefully trace the pattern onto template plastic, making sure to label the template and to transfer any alignment or grain line markings. Cut out template along drawn line. Check your template against the original pattern for accuracy.

MACHINE APPLIQUÉ
Preparing Fusible Appliqués

Patterns for fused appliqués are printed in reverse to enable you to use our speedy method of preparing appliqués. White or light-colored fabrics may need to be lined with fusible interfacing before applying fusible web to prevent darker fabrics from showing through.

1. Place paper-backed fusible web, web side down, over appliqué pattern. Use a pencil to trace pattern onto paper side of web as many times as indicated in project instructions for a single fabric. Repeat for additional patterns and fabrics.
2. Follow manufacturer's instructions to fuse traced patterns to wrong side of fabrics. Do not remove paper backing. (**Note:** Some pieces may be given as measurements, such as a 2" x 4" rectangle, instead of drawn patterns. Fuse web to wrong side of the fabrics indicated for these pieces.)
3. Use scissors to cut out appliqué pieces along traced lines; use rotary cutting equipment to cut out appliqué pieces given as measurements. Remove paper backing from all pieces.

Invisible Appliqué

This machine appliqué method uses clear nylon thread to secure the appliqué pieces. Transparent monofilament (clear nylon) thread is available in 2 colors: clear and smoke. Use clear on white or very light fabrics and smoke on darker colors.

1. Referring to diagram and/or photo, arrange prepared appliqués on the background fabric and follow manufacturer's instructions to fuse in place.
2. Pin a stabilizer, such as paper or any of the commercially available products, on wrong side of background fabric before stitching appliqués in place.
3. Thread sewing machine with transparent monofilament thread; use general-purpose thread that matches background fabric in bobbin.
4. Set sewing machine for a very narrow width (approximately ¹⁄₁₆") zigzag stitch and a short stitch length. You may find that loosening the top tension slightly will yield a smoother stitch.
5. Begin by stitching 2 or 3 stitches in place (drop feed dogs or set stitch length at 0) to anchor thread. Most of the zigzag stitch should be done on the appliqué with the right edges of the stitch falling at the very outside edge of the appliqué. Stitch over all exposed raw edges of appliqué pieces.
6. (**Note:** Dots on **Figs. 10-15** indicate where to leave needle in fabric when pivoting.) For **outside corners**, stitch just past the corner, stopping with the needle in **background** fabric (**Fig. 10**). Raise presser foot. Pivot project, lower presser foot, and stitch adjacent side (**Fig. 11**).

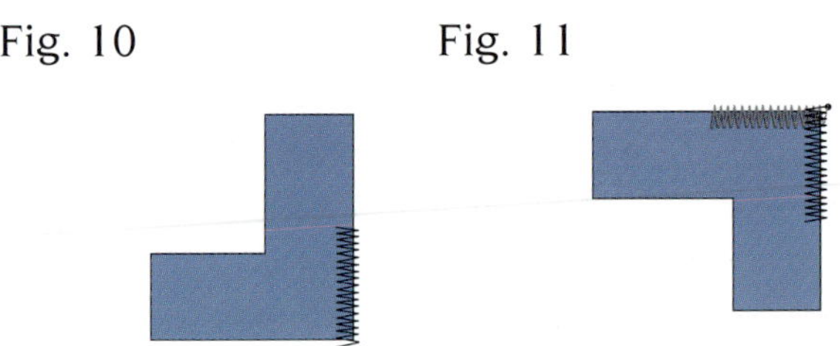

Fig. 10   Fig. 11

7. For **inside corners**, stitch just past the corner, stopping with the needle in **appliqué** fabric (**Fig. 12**). Raise presser foot. Pivot project, lower presser foot, and stitch adjacent side (**Fig. 13**).

Fig. 12   Fig. 13

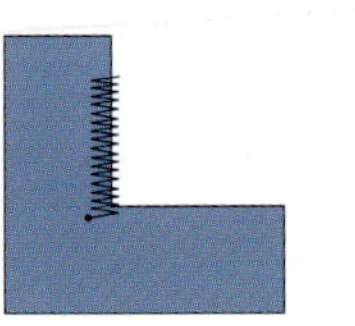
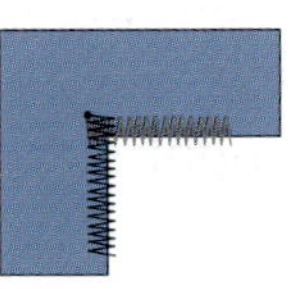

8. When stitching **outside** curves, stop with needle in **background** fabric. Raise presser foot and pivot project as needed. Lower presser foot and continue stitching, pivoting as often as necessary to follow curve (**Fig. 14**).

Fig. 14

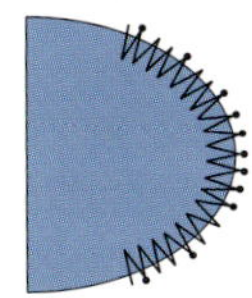

9. When stitching **inside** curves, stop with needle in **appliqué** fabric. Raise presser foot and pivot project as needed. Lower presser foot and continue stitching, pivoting as often as necessary to follow curve (**Fig. 15**).

Fig. 15

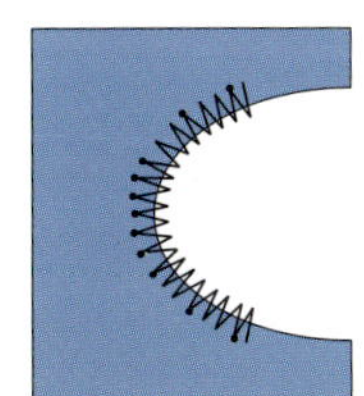

10. Do not backstitch at end of stitching. Pull threads to wrong side of background fabric; knot thread and trim ends.
11. Carefully tear away stabilizer.

Mock Hand Appliqué

This stitch uses the blind stitch on your sewing machine to achieve a look that closely resembles traditional hand appliqué. Using an updated method, appliqués are prepared with turned-under edges and then machine stitched to the background fabric. For best appliqué results, your sewing machine must have blind stitch capability with a variable stitch width. If your blind stitch width cannot be adjusted, you may still wish to try this technique to see if you are happy with the results. Some sewing machines have a narrower blind stitch width than others.

1. Matching right sides, place appliqué fabric and a piece of lightweight cotton fabric together. Trace around template on wrong side of cotton fabric. Stitch on drawn line. Use pinking shears to trim seam allowance to ⅛". To make opening for turning, cut a slit in cotton fabric only (**Fig. 16**). Turn right side out and press to make appliqué.

Fig. 16

2. Thread needle of sewing machine with transparent monofilament thread; use general-purpose thread in bobbin in a color to match background fabric.
3. Set sewing machine for narrow blind stitch (just wide enough to catch 2 or 3 threads of the appliqué) and a very short stitch length (20-30 stitches per inch).
4. Arrange appliqué pieces on background fabric as described in project instructions. Use pins or hand baste to secure.
5. (*Note:* Follow Steps 6-9 of **Invisible Appliqué**, pages 52-53, for needle position when pivoting.) Sew around edges of each appliqué so that the straight stitches fall on the background fabric very near the appliqué and the "hem" stitches barely catch the folded edge of the appliqué (**Fig. 17**).

Fig. 17

6. It is not necessary to backstitch at the beginning or end of stitching. End stitching by sewing ¼" over the first stitches. Trim thread ends close to fabric.

Satin Stitch Appliqué

A good satin stitch is a thick, smooth, almost solid line of zigzag stitching that covers the exposed raw edges of appliqué pieces.

1. Follow Steps 1 and 2 of **Invisible Appliqué**, page 52.

2. Thread needle of sewing machine with general-purpose thread. Use thread that matches the background fabric in the bobbin for all stitching. Set sewing machine for a medium width zigzag stitch (approximately $^1/_8$") and a very short stitch length. Set upper tension slightly looser than for regular stitching. Refer to Steps 5-11 of **Invisible Appliqué**, pages 52- 53 to stitch appliqués in place.

BORDERS

Borders cut along the lengthwise grain will lie flatter than borders cut along the crosswise grain. Cutting lengths given for borders in this book are exact. You may wish to add an extra 2" of length at each end for "insurance"; borders will be trimmed after measuring completed center section of quilt top.

Adding Squared Borders

1. Mark the center of each edge of quilt top.
2. Most of the borders in this book have the side borders added first. To add side borders, measure across center of quilt top to determine length of borders (**Fig. 18**). Trim side borders to the determined length.

Fig. 18

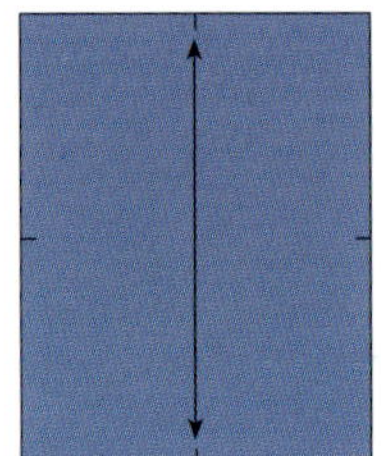

3. Mark center of one long edge of side border. Matching center marks and raw edges, pin border to quilt top, easing in any fullness; stitch. Repeat for other side border.
4. Measure center of quilt top, including attached borders, to determine length of top and bottom borders. Trim top and bottom borders to the determined length. Repeat Step 3 to add borders to quilt top (**Fig. 19**).

Fig. 19

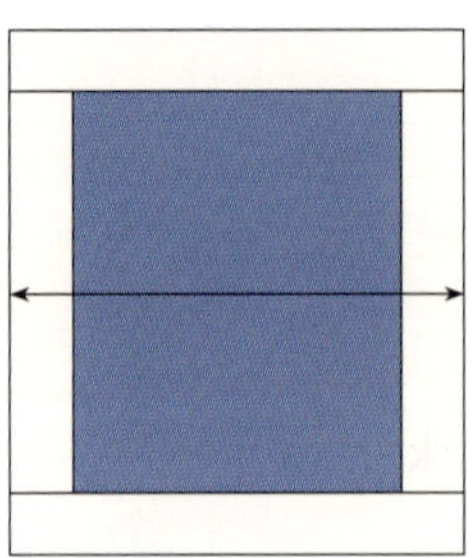

QUILTING

Quilting holds the 3 layers (top, batting, and backing) of the quilt together and can be done by hand or machine. Our project instructions tell you which method is used on each project. Because marking, layering, and quilting are interrelated and may be done in different orders depending on circumstances, please read the entire **Quilting** *section, pages 54 - 57, before beginning the quilting process on your project.*

Types Of Quilting
In the Ditch Quilting

Quilting very close to a seamline or appliqué is called "in the ditch" quilting. This type of quilting does not need to be marked. When quilting in the ditch, quilt on the side **opposite** the seam allowance.

Outline Quilting

Quilting approximately $^1/_4$" from a seam or appliqué is called "outline" quilting. Outline quilting may be marked, or you may place $^1/_4$"w masking tape along seamlines and quilt along the opposite edge of the tape. (Do not leave tape on quilt longer than necessary, since it may leave an adhesive residue.)

Marking Quilting Lines

Fabric marking pencils, various types of chalk markers, and fabric marking pens with inks that disappear with exposure to air or water are readily available and work well for different applications. Lead pencils work well on light-color fabrics, but marks may be difficult to remove. White pencils work well on dark-color fabrics, and silver pencils show up well on many colors. Since chalk rubs off easily, it's a good choice if you are marking as you quilt. Fabric marking pens make more durable and visible markings, but the marks should be carefully removed according to manufacturer's instructions. Press down only as hard as necessary to make a visible line.

When you choose to mark your quilt, whether before or after the layers are basted together, is also a factor in deciding which marking tool to use. If you mark with chalk or a chalk pencil, handling the quilt during basting may rub off the markings. Intricate or ornamental designs may not be practical to mark as you quilt; mark these designs before basting using a more durable marker.

To choose marking tools, take all these factors into consideration and test different markers on scrap fabric until you find the one that gives the desired result.

Choosing and Preparing the Backing

To allow for slight shifting of the quilt top during quilting, the backing should be approximately 4" larger on all sides for a bed-size quilt top or approximately 2" larger on all sides for a wall hanging. Yardage requirements listed for quilt backings are calculated for 45"w fabric. If you are making a bed-size quilt, using 90"w or 108"w fabric for the backing may eliminate piecing. To piece a backing using 45"w fabric, use the following instructions.

1. Measure length and width of quilt top; add 8" (4" for a wall hanging) to each measurement.
2. If quilt top is 76"w or less, cut backing fabric into 2 lengths slightly longer than the determined length measurement. Trim selvages. Place lengths with right sides facing and sew long edges together, forming a tube (**Fig. 20**). Match seams and press along 1 fold (**Fig. 21**). Cut along pressed fold to form a single piece (**Fig. 22**).

Fig. 20	Fig. 21	Fig. 22

3. If quilt top is more than 76"w, cut backing fabric into 3 lengths slightly longer than the determined width measurement. Trim selvages. Sew long edges together to form a single piece.

4. Trim backing to correct size, if necessary, and press seam allowances open.

Choosing and Preparing the Batting

Choosing the right batting will make your quilting job easier. For fine hand quilting, choose a low-loft batting in any of the fiber types described here. Machine quilters will want to choose a low-loft batting that is all cotton or a cotton/polyester blend because the cotton helps "grip" the layers of the quilt. If the quilt is to be tied, a high-loft batting, sometimes called extra-loft or fat batting, is a good choice.

Batting is available in many different fibers. Bonded polyester batting is one of the most popular batting types. It is treated with a protective coating to stabilize the fibers and to reduce "bearding," a process in which batting fibers work their way out through the quilt fabrics. Other batting options include cotton/polyester batting, which combines the best of both polyester and cotton battings; all-cotton batting, which must be quilted more closely than polyester batting; and wool and silk battings, which are generally more expensive and usually only dry-cleanable.

Whichever batting you choose, read the manufacturer's instructions closely for any special notes on care or preparation. When you're ready to use your chosen batting in a project, cut batting the same size as the prepared backing.

Assembling the Quilt

1. Examine wrong side of quilt top closely; trim any seam allowances and clip any threads that may show through the front of the quilt. Press quilt top.
2. If quilt top is to be marked before layering, mark quilting lines (see **Marking Quilting Lines**, page 54).
3. Place backing **wrong** side up on a flat surface. Use masking tape to tape edges of backing to surface. Place batting on top of backing fabric. Smooth batting gently, being careful not to stretch or tear. Center quilt top right side up on batting.

4. If hand quilting, begin in the center and work toward the outer edges to hand baste all layers together. Use long stitches and place basting lines approximately 4" apart (**Fig. 23**). Smooth fullness or wrinkles toward outer edges.

Fig. 23

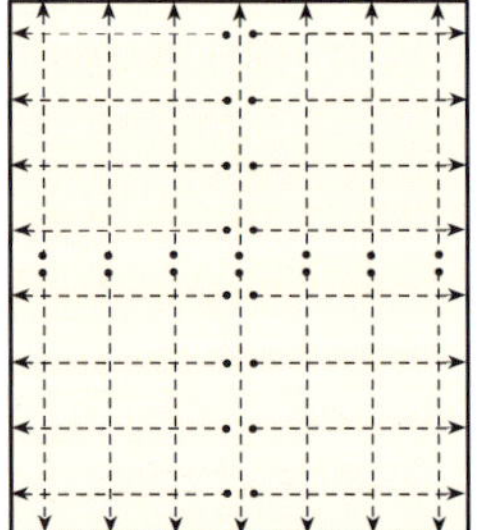

5. If machine quilting, use 1" rustproof safety pins to "pin-baste" all layers together, spacing pins approximately 4" apart. Begin at the center and work toward the outer edges to secure all layers. If possible, place pins away from areas that will be quilted, although pins may be removed as needed when quilting.

Hand Quilting

The quilting stitch is a basic running stitch that forms a broken line on the quilt top and backing. Stitches on the quilt top and backing should be straight and equal in length.

1. Secure center of quilt in hoop or frame. Check quilt top and backing to make sure they are smooth. To help prevent puckers, always begin quilting in the center of the quilt and work toward the outside edges.
2. Thread needle with an 18"-20" length of quilting thread; knot 1 end. Using a thimble, insert needle into quilt top and batting approximately $1/2$" from where you wish to begin quilting. Bring needle up at the point where you wish to begin (**Fig. 24**); when knot catches on quilt top, give thread a quick, short pull to "pop" knot through fabric into batting (**Fig. 25**).

Fig. 24

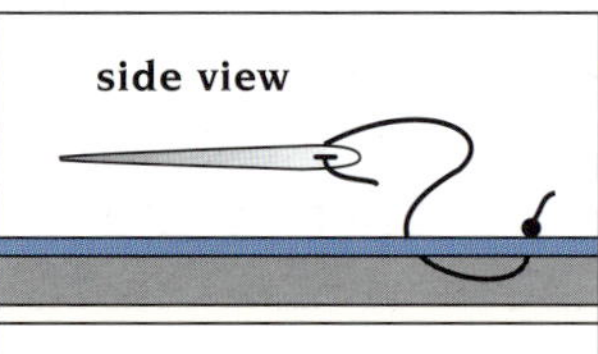

Fig. 25

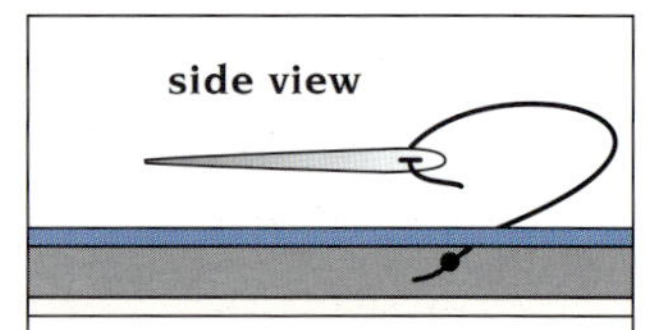

3. Holding the needle with your sewing hand and placing your other hand underneath the quilt, use thimble to push the tip of the needle down through all layers. As soon as needle touches your finger underneath, use that finger to push the tip of the needle only back up through the layers to top of quilt. (The amount of the needle showing above the fabric determines the length of the quilting stitch.) Referring to **Fig. 26**, rock the needle up and down, taking 3 - 6 stitches before bringing the needle and thread completely through the layers. Check the back of the quilt to make sure stitches are going through all layers. When quilting through a seam allowance or quilting a curve or corner, you may need to make 1 stitch at a time.

Fig. 26

4. When you reach the end of your thread, knot thread close to the fabric and "pop" knot into batting; clip thread close to fabric.
5. Stop and move your hoop as often as necessary. You do not have to tie a knot every time you move your hoop; you may leave the thread dangling and pick it up again when you return to that part of the quilt.

Machine Quilting

The following instructions are for straight-line quilting, which requires a walking foot or even-feed foot. The term "straight-line" is somewhat deceptive, since curves (especially gentle ones) as well as straight lines can be stitched with this technique.

1. Wind your sewing machine bobbin with general-purpose thread that matches the quilt backing. Do not use quilting thread. Thread the needle of your machine with transparent monofilament thread if you want your quilting to blend with your quilt top fabrics. Use decorative thread, such as a metallic or contrasting-color general-purpose thread, when you want the quilting lines to stand out more. Set the stitch length for 6 - 10 stitches per inch and attach the walking foot to sewing machine.

2. After pin-basting, decide which section of the quilt will have the longest continuous quilting line, oftentimes the area from center top to center bottom. Leaving the area exposed where you will place your first line of quilting, roll up each edge of the quilt to help reduce the bulk, keeping fabrics smooth. Smaller projects may not need to be rolled.

3. Start stitching at beginning of longest quilting line, using very short stitches for the first $1/4$" to "lock" beginning of quilting line. Stitch across project, using one hand on each side of the walking foot to slightly spread the fabric and to guide the fabric through the machine. Lock stitches at end of quilting line.

4. Continue machine quilting, stitching longer quilting lines first to stabilize the quilt before moving on to other areas.

Machine Stipple Quilting

The term, "stipple quilting," refers to dense quilting using a meandering line of machine stitching or closely spaced hand stitching.

1. Wind your sewing machine bobbin with general-purpose thread that matches the quilt backing. Do not use quilting thread. Thread the needle of your machine with transparent monofilament thread if you want your quilting to blend with your quilt top fabrics. Use decorative thread, such as a metallic or contrasting-colored general-purpose thread, when you want the quilting lines to stand out more.

2. For random stipple quilting, use a darning foot, drop or cover feed dogs, and set stitch length at zero. Pull up bobbin thread and hold both thread ends while you stitch 2 or 3 stitches in place to lock thread. Cut threads near quilt surface. Place hands lightly on quilt on either side of darning foot.

3. Begin stitching in a meandering pattern (**Fig. 27**), guiding the quilt with your hands. The object is to make stitches of similar length and to not sew over previous stitching lines. The movement of your hands is what determines the stitch length; it takes practice to coordinate your hand motions and the pressure you put on the foot pedal, so go slowly at first.

Fig. 27

4. Continue machine quilting, filling in one open area of the quilt before moving on to another area, locking thread again at end of each line of stitching by sewing 2 or 3 stitches in place and trimming thread ends.

BINDING

Binding encloses the raw edges of your quilt. Because of its stretchiness, bias binding works well for binding projects with curves or rounded corners and tends to lie smooth and flat in any given circumstance. It is also more durable than other types of binding.

Making Continuous Bias Strip Binding

Bias strips for binding can simply be cut and pieced to the desired length. However, when a long length of binding is needed, the "continuous" method is quick and accurate.

1. Cut a square from binding fabric the size indicated in the project instructions. Cut square in half diagonally to make 2 triangles.

2. With right sides together and using a $1/4$" seam allowance, sew triangles together (**Fig. 28**); press seam allowance open.

Fig. 28

3. On wrong side of fabric, draw lines the width of the binding as specified in the project instructions, usually 2¹/₂" (**Fig. 29**). Cut off any remaining fabric less than this width.

Fig. 29

4. With right sides inside, bring short edges together to form a tube; match raw edges so that first drawn line of top section meets second drawn line of bottom section (**Fig. 30**).

Fig. 30

5. Carefully pin edges together by inserting pins through drawn lines at the point where drawn lines intersect, making sure the pins go through intersections on both sides. Using a ¹/₄" seam allowance, sew edges together. Press seam allowance open.
6. To cut continuous strip, begin cutting along first drawn line (**Fig. 31**). Continue cutting along drawn line around tube.

Fig. 31

7. Trim ends of bias strip square.
8. Matching wrong sides and raw edges, press bias strip in half lengthwise to complete binding.

Making Straight-Grain Binding

Binding may also be cut from the straight lengthwise or crosswise grain of the fabric. You will find that straight-grain binding works well for small projects and projects with straight edges.

1. Measure each edge of quilt; add 3" to each measurement. Cut lengthwise or crosswise strips of binding fabric the width called for in the project instructions. Strips may be pieced to achieve the necessary length.
2. Matching wrong sides and raw edges, press binding in half lengthwise.

Attaching Binding With Mitered Corners

1. Press 1 end of binding diagonally (**Fig. 32**).

Fig. 32

2. Beginning with pressed end several inches from a corner, lay binding around quilt to make sure that seams in binding will not end up at a corner. Adjust placement if necessary. Matching raw edges of binding to raw edge of quilt top, pin binding to right side of quilt along 1 edge.
3. When you reach the first corner, mark ¹/₄" from corner of quilt top (**Fig. 33**).

Fig. 33

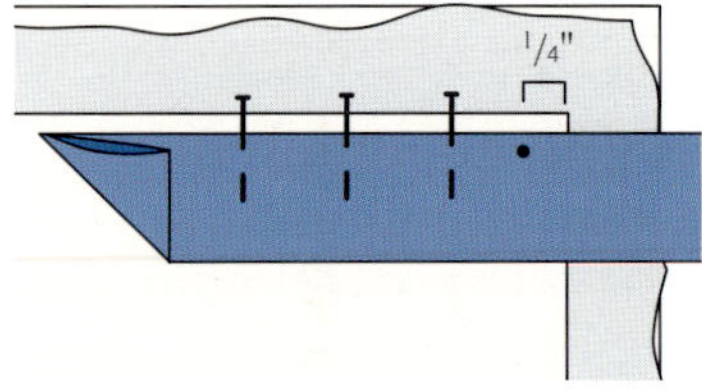

4. Using a ¹/₄" seam allowance, sew binding to quilt, backstitching at beginning of stitching and when you reach the mark (**Fig. 34**). Lift needle out of fabric and clip thread.

Fig. 34

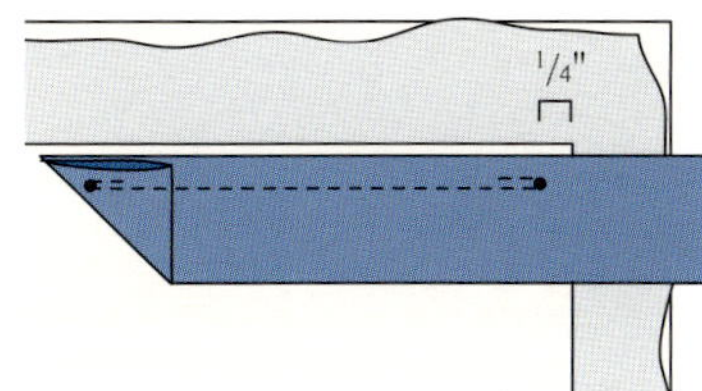

5. Fold binding as shown in **Figs. 35** and **36** and pin binding to adjacent side, matching raw edges. When you reach the next corner, mark $^1/_4$" from edge of quilt top.

Fig. 35   Fig. 36

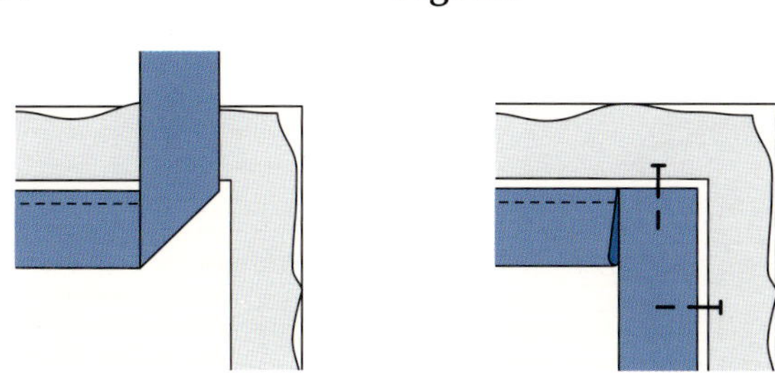

6. Backstitching at edge of quilt top, sew pinned binding to quilt (**Fig. 37**); backstitch when you reach the next mark. Lift needle out of fabric and clip thread.

Fig. 37

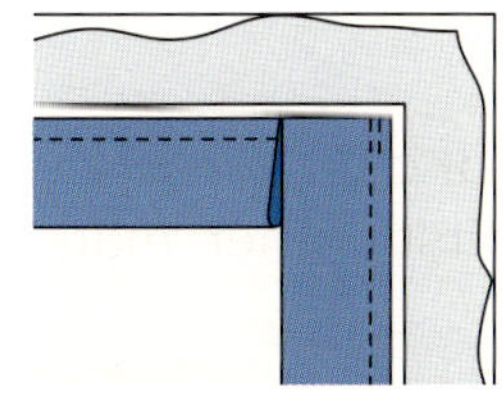

7. Repeat Steps 5 and 6 to continue sewing binding to quilt until binding overlaps beginning end by approximately 2". Trim excess binding.
8. If using $2^1/_2$"w binding (finished size $^1/_2$"), trim backing and batting a scant $^1/_4$" larger than quilt top so that batting and backing will fill the binding when it is folded over to the quilt backing. If using narrower binding, trim backing and batting even with edges of quilt top.

9. On 1 edge of quilt, fold binding over to quilt backing and pin pressed edge in place, covering stitching line (**Fig. 38**). On adjacent side, fold binding over, forming a mitered corner (**Fig. 39**). Repeat to pin remainder of binding in place.

Fig. 38   Fig. 39

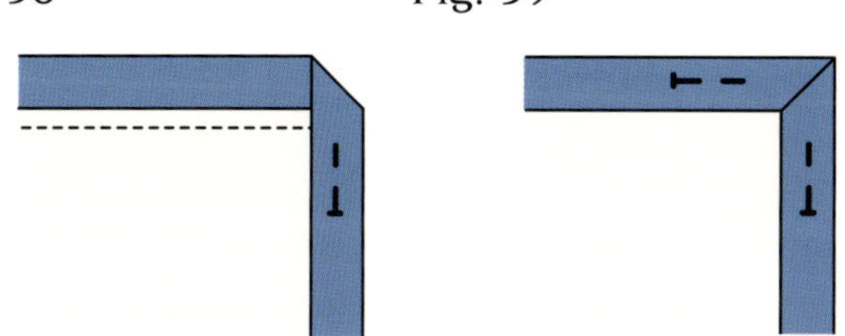

10. Blind stitch binding to backing, taking care not to stitch through to front of quilt.

Blind Stitch
Come up at 1. Go down at 2 and come up at 3. Length of stitches may be varied as desired.

Fig. 40

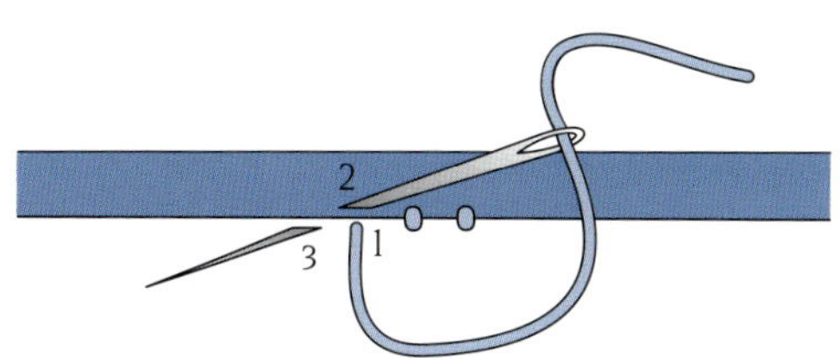

Metric Conversion Chart

Inches x 2.54 = centimeters (cm)	Yards x .9144 = meters (m)
Inches x 25.4 = millimeters (mm)	Yards x 91.44 = centimeters (cm)
Inches x .0254 = meters (m)	Centimeters x .3937 = inches (")
	Meters x 1.0936 = yards (yd)

Standard Equivalents

$^1/_8$"	3.2 mm	0.32 cm	$^1/_8$ yard	11.43 cm	0.11 m
$^1/_4$"	6.35 mm	0.635 cm	$^1/_4$ yard	22.86 cm	0.23 m
$^3/_8$"	9.5 mm	0.95 cm	$^3/_8$ yard	34.29 cm	0.34 m
$^1/_2$"	12.7 mm	1.27 cm	$^1/_2$ yard	45.72 cm	0.46 m
$^5/_8$"	15.9 mm	1.59 cm	$^5/_8$ yard	57.15 cm	0.57 m
$^3/_4$"	19.1 mm	1.91 cm	$^3/_4$ yard	68.58 cm	0.69 m
$^7/_8$"	22.2 mm	2.22 cm	$^7/_8$ yard	80 cm	0.8 m
1"	25.4 mm	2.54 cm	1 yard	91.44 cm	0.91 m

Machine quilting by The Quilter's Loft of DeKalb, IL, 1-877-999-8233.

We have made every effort to ensure that these instructions are accurate and complete. We cannot, however, be responsible for human error, typographical mistakes, or variations in individual work.

Production Team: Technical Writer – Andrea Ahlen; Editorial Writer – Susan McManus Johnson; Graphic Artists- Jenny Dickerson and Stephanie Hamling